Strategic Intelligence and Beyond

MW00811402

Strategic Intelligence in the Cold War and Beyond looks at the many events, personalities, and controversies in the field of intelligence and espionage since the end of World War II. A crucial but often neglected topic, strategic intelligence took on added significance during the protracted struggle of the Cold War.

In this accessible volume, Jefferson Adams places these important developments in their historical context, taking a global approach to themes including:

- various undertakings from both sides in the Cold War, with emphasis on covert action and deception operations;
- controversial episodes involving Cuba, Chile, Nicaragua, Vietnam, Poland, and Afghanistan, as well as numerous lesser known occurrences;
- three Cold War spy profiles which explore the role of human psychology in intelligence work;
- the technological dimension;
- spies in fiction, film, and television;
- developments in the intelligence organizations of both sides in the decade following the fall of the Berlin Wall.

Supplemented by suggestions for further reading, a glossary of key terms, and a timeline of important events, this is an essential read for all those interested in the modern history of espionage.

Jefferson Adams is Professor of European History at Sarah Lawrence College. His publications include *Beyond the Wall: Memoirs of an East and West German Spy* (ed., 1992) and *Historical Dictionary of German Intelligence* (2009). He is also the senior editor of *The International Journal of Intelligence and Counterintelligence*.

The Making of the Contemporary World
Edited by Eric J. Evans and Ruth Henig

The Making of the Contemporary World series provides challenging interpretations of contemporary issues and debates within strongly defined historical frameworks. The range of the series is global, with each volume drawing together material from numerous disciplines – including economics, politics, and sociology. The books in this series present compact, indispensable introductions for students studying the modern world.

Strategic Intelligence in the Cold War and Beyond

Jefferson Adams

Routledge
Taylor & Francis Group

LONDON AND NEW YORK

First published 2015
by Routledge
2 Park Square, Milton Park, Abingdon, Oxon OX14 4RN

and published by Routledge
711 Third Avenue, New York, NY 10017

Routledge is an imprint of the Taylor & Francis Group, an informa business

British Library Cataloguing in Publication Data
A catalogue record for this book is available from the British Library

Library of Congress Cataloging in Publication Data
Adams, Jefferson.
Strategic intelligence in the Cold War and beyond / Jefferson Adams.
pages cm. -- (The making of the contemporary world)
Includes bibliographical references and index.
1. Intelligence service--History. 2. Military intelligence--History. 3. Espionage--History. 4. Spies--History. 5. Cold War. I. Title.
JF1525.I6A34 2014
327.1209--dc23
2014006326

ISBN: 978-0-415-78206-7 (hbk)
ISBN: 978-0-415-78207-4 (pbk)
ISBN: 978-1-315-75894-7 (ebk)

Typeset in Times New Roman
by Taylor & Francis Books

Contents

Abbreviations

AFL-CIO	American Federation of Labor-Congress of Industrial Organizations (US)
AfNS	Amt für Nationale Sicherheit (East German Office for National Security)
AVO/AVH	Államvédelmi Osztály/Államvédelmi Hatosag (Hungarian Security and Intelligence Service)
BfV	Bundesamt für Verfassungsschutz (West German/German Federal Office for the Protection of the Constitution)
BIS	Bezpečnostní informační služba (Czech Republic Security Information Service)
BND	Bundesnachrichtendienst (West German/German Federal Intelligence Service)
BStU	Bundesbeauftragten für die Unterlagen des Staatssicherheitsdienstes der ehemaligen Deutschen Demokratischen Republik (Federal Commissioner for the Records of the State Security Service of the former German Democratic Republic/Gauck Authority)
Cheka	Vserossiiskaya Chrezvychainaya Komissiya po Borbe s Kontrrevolyutsiei i Sabotazhem (All-Russian Extraordinary Commission for Combating Counter-Revolution and Sabotage)
CIA	Central Intelligence Agency (US)
CIS	Commonwealth of Independent States
CPUSA	Communist Party USA
DCI	director of central intelligence (US)
DGI	Dirección General de Inteligencia (Cuban Intelligence Service)
DGSE	Direction Générale de la Sécurité Extérieure (French Foreign Intelligence Service)

DIE	Departamentul de Informatii Externe (Romanian Foreign Intelligence Service)
DS	Durzhavna Sigurnost (Bulgarian Security and Intelligence Service)
DST	Direction de la Surveillance du Territoire (French Domestic Security Service)
EU	European Union
FBI	Federal Bureau of Investigation (US)
FHO	Fremde Heere Ost (Foreign Armies East – Germany)
FRG	Federal Republic of Germany
FSB	Federalnaya Sluzhba Bezopasnosti (Russian Federal Security Service)
FSK	Federal'naia Sluzhba Kontrrazvedki (Russian Federal Counterintelligence Service)
FSLN	Frente Sandinista de Liberación Nacional (Sandinistas)
GDR	German Democratic Republic
GRU	Glavnoye Razvedyvatel'noye Upravieniye (Main Intelligence Directorate of the Soviet General Staff)
HUMINT	intelligence derived from human sources
HVA	Hauptverwaltung Aufklärung (East German Foreign Intelligence Service)
KGB	Komitet Gosudarstvennoy Bezopasnosti (Soviet Committee of State Security)
KI	Komitet Informatsii (Soviet Committee of Information)
MACVSOG:	Military Assistance Command Vietnam Studies and Observation Unit
MB	Ministestvo Bezopastnosti (Russian Ministry of Security)
MfS	Ministerium für Staatssicherheit (East German Ministry of State Security)
MGB	Ministerstvo Gosudarstvennoi Bezopasnosti (First Directorate of the Soviet State Security/Soviet Ministry of State Security)
MI5	Security Service (UK)
MI6	alternate designation for SIS (UK)
MICE	money, ideology, career, and ego
MSS	Guoanbu (Ministry of State Security of the People's Republic of China)
NATO	North Atlantic Treaty Organization

NBH	Nemzetbiztonsagi Hivatal (Hungarian National Security Office)
NBSzSz	Nemzetbiztonsagi Szakszolgalat (Hungarian National Security Service)
NKVD	Narodnyy Komissariat Vnutrennikh Del (Soviet People's Commissariat of Internal Affairs)
NSA	National Security Agency (US)
NSC	National Security Council (US)
NKGB/MGB	Narodniy Kommissariat Gosudarstevennoi Bezopasnosti/Ministerstsvo Gosudarstevennoi Bezopastnosti (Soviet People's Commissariat of State Security/Ministry of State Security)
OG	Organisation Gehlen (Gehlen Organization/West German Foreign Intelligence Agency)
OPC	Office of Policy Coordination (US)
OSS	Office of Strategic Services (US)
PCF	Parti communiste français (French Communist Party)
PDPA	People's Democratic Party of Afghanistan
PRC	People's Republic of China
PSIA	*koanchosa-cho* (Japanese Public Security Investigative Agency)
RFE/RL	Radio Free Europe/Radio Liberty (US)
SB	Sluzba Bezpieczenstw (Polish Security and Intelligence Service)
SDECE	Service de Documentation Extérieure et de Contre-espionage (French Foreign Intelligence Service)
SED	Sozialistische Einheitspartei Deutschlands (German Socialist Unity Party)
SHAI	Sherut ha' Yediot ha'Artzit (Israeli National Information Service)
SIE	Serviciul de Informatlii Externe (Romanian Foreign Intelligence Service)
SIGINT	intelligence derived from interception and analysis of signals
SIS	Secret Intelligence Service (UK)/ Slovenská informačná služba (Slovak Information Service)
SOE	Special Operations Executive (UK)
SPD	Sozialdemokratische Partei Deutschlands (Social Democratic Party of Germany)
SRI	Servicul Roman de Infortli (Romanian Security Service)

SS	Schutzstaffel (Nazi Party Protection Squadrons)
Stasi	Ministerium für Staatssicherheit (East German Ministry of State Security)
StB	Státni Bezpecnost (Czechoslovakian Security and Intelligence Service)
SVR	Sluzhba Vnesheni Razvedki (Russian Foreign Intelligence Service)
UN	United Nations
UOP	Urzad Ochrony Panstwa (Polish State Protection Office)
ÚZSI	Úřad pro zahraniční styky a informace (Czech Republic Foreign Intelligence Service)

Perception is strong and sight weak. In strategy it is important to see distant things as they were close and to take a distanced view of close things.

Miyamoto Musashi, a seventeenth-century
Japanese swordsman

1 Introduction

Strategic intelligence on a broad front lay at the heart of countless struggles waged during the Cold War. Some have called it the secret war in the Cold War. One historian has fittingly characterized the intelligence networks of this era as its "light infantry" – the only force that could be mobilized given the nuclear stalemate that had developed between the superpowers.[1] Yet, unfortunately, too many accounts dealing with this period persist in ignoring the vital dimension of intelligence, preferring to concentrate almost solely on the political and diplomatic maneuverings of the major adversaries. When the subject of espionage is broached, one often encounters a glaring asymmetry: on the one hand, frequent references to the activities of the Central Intelligence Agency (CIA) – notably in the Third World – but, on the other, few if any regarding Soviet and Eastern bloc intelligence operations. Besides providing a general introduction to the topic, this volume is intended to help correct this imbalance. It also extends the time frame to examine post-Cold War developments in the decade following the fall of the Berlin Wall.

For most laypersons, matters involving intelligence tend to be reduced to images of covert action – the toppling of an unfriendly foreign government or supplying under-the-table subsidies to ostensibly independent groups or individuals. The field of intelligence, however, is multifaceted and comprised of various distinct components such as research and analysis, counterintelligence, and cryptography. Each has a separate methodology, and each tends to develop its own *esprit de corps*, if not rivalry with other intelligence branches. A former CIA analyst referred to a "bureaucratic Berlin Wall" that separated his branch from the clandestine service, except at the uppermost levels.[2] Seen in monetary terms, it is striking that the budget of the National Security Agency (NSA), charged with safeguarding the US government's communications network, easily eclipses the allotment received by the CIA. Of those funds, covert action receives only a small percentage. Altogether the US intelligence community encompasses 17 agencies and organizations within the executive branch of the government.

Despite countless attempts to formulate an all-embracing theory by scholars and practitioners alike, intelligence work defies a positivist or scientific approach. The analyst is often grappling with ambiguous and fragmentary evidence and must weigh its validity in the context of the prevailing threat level. The same piece of information might be accorded a high degree of relevance if a potential attack were deemed imminent or basically discounted should that not be the case. And as classified reports move through the large secret service bureaucracies, they are subject to constant review and evaluation. Hard inconvertible facts, as a result, rarely exist on their own. In addition, the successful recruitment of an informant usually depends upon a keen intuitive understanding of the individual involved. In fact, real life espionage, full of unexpected twists and turns, can easily trigger some of the most bizarre examples of human behavior. Were some of these incidents submitted in fictional form to a publishing house, they would likely be rejected as simply too implausible. What the American spymaster Allen Dulles once dubbed as "the craft of intelligence" seems as apt a characterization as any that has ever been advanced. He further added that it is "probably the least understood and the most misrepresented of the professions."[3]

There is inevitably the crucial question of sources. How, many ask, can one know what really transpired in the shadowy realm of espionage? Reasons for skepticism clearly abound. So often confidential exchanges are purposely conducted orally in order not to leave a domestic paper trail or run the risk of being monitored by an enemy service. An old intelligence axiom holds that "if you want to keep it secret, don't write it down." Documents themselves can be difficult to obtain from government archives, particularly given the ever-present tension between historians desiring to reconstruct as complete a picture of the past as possible and state officials wary of releasing materials that could compromise individuals or methods. In the case of the Cold War, the Russian archives present a most formidable obstacle. Neither the KGB nor the Soviet Military Intelligence (GRU) archives have been made available for general inquiry. According to Moscow's highly manipulative procedures, only certain batches of documents, often extracted from their historical context, tend to be shown to selected researchers. A special fee might even be imposed, and an appropriate KGB co-author assigned to the project.

Still, the historian need not despair. In the wake of the Watergate affair, Congress expanded the Freedom of Information Act in 1974, which has permitted access to many files of the Federal Bureau of Investigation for the first time, while an executive order issued in 1982 has given individual researchers and former presidential appointees the possibility of examining classified documents of the CIA. Open sources, too, can provide a unique and often underappreciated window into the world of intelligence. Such was the experience of those academics assigned to the Research and Analysis Division of the Office of Strategic Services during World War II. Much to the surprise of the military commanders, these specialists managed to ascertain key changes in the enemy's disposition of resources by closely perusing scholarly works, specialized journals, and foreign newspapers and magazines. In another instance, the historian Richard Pipes, while assigned to the National Security Council in the early 1980s, found that the *Intelligence Daily* that landed on his desk every morning added little to what he had already read in the world press. From his vantage point, it was difficult not to conclude that classified data rarely outweighs what can be found in the public domain. More recently, a CIA analyst noted that nearly 60 percent of the sources utilized by his technical branch originated in scientific journals, computer databases, newspaper reports, and translated items by the agency's Foreign Broadcast Information Service.[4] Other analysts place the figure closer to 80 percent in their work.

In the meantime, a number of former Soviet intelligence officers fled safely to the West, bringing with them their detailed memories relating to what had transpired at the upper levels of decision-making in Moscow. When Oleg Gordievsky made his escape from Moscow in 1985, he departed with a wealth of information on the KGB's operations, personnel, and organizational structure. In another extraordinary instance, Vasili Mitrokhin even managed to bring an entire archive with him to Britain in 1992 – ten manuscript volumes of daily notes that he secretly made while covering a 12-year period working in the KGB's foreign intelligence branch. An invaluable source regarding Soviet espionage in the United States have been the notebooks of Alexander Vassiliev, a Moscow journalist and ex-KGB officer who was given privileged access to archival holdings a year after the demise of the Soviet Union as part of a large-scale book project. Then, too, there is the case of the former German Democratic Republic, whose total collapse at the end of the Cold War created the unprecedented opportunity to examine the surviving voluminous records of its powerful and seemingly ubiquitous state security apparatus.

Sometimes a lengthy time lag may be involved. Not until the early 1970s – more than 25 years following the end of World War II – did the story reach the general public of how Ultra and Bletchley Park overcame enormous odds and defeated the sophisticated German Enigma cipher machine. Or in another classic code-breaking feat, the Venona decryptions of Soviet intelligence traffic during the period 1942–1949 remained highly classified information by the US government until after the end of the Cold War. What therefore follows in these pages reflects the painstaking research of many scholars in the field of intelligence – particularly since 1989 – with the important proviso that more revelations about the Cold War period will doubtlessly see the future light of day.

Notes

1 Vladislav M. Zubov, "Spy vs. Spy: The KGB vs. the CIA, 1960–62," in *Cold War International History Project Bulletin* (Washington, DC: Woodrow Wilson Center for Scholars), no. 4, 22.
2 Robert M. Gates, *From the Shadows: The Ultimate Insider's Story of Five Presidents and How They Won the Cold War* (New York, NY: Simon and Schuster, 1996), 33–34.
3 Allen Dulles, *The Craft of Intelligence* (New York, NY: Harper and Row, 1963), 5.
4 Loch K. Johnson, *Secret Agencies: US Intelligence in a Hostile World* (New Haven, CT: Yale University Press, 1996), 4.

2   The Players

One of the defining moments following the end of World War II was the decision of President Harry S. Truman to sign the National Defense Act on July 26, 1947. This piece of legislation brought the Central Intelligence Agency (CIA) into official existence, thus ending several years of acrimonious debate. Such an organization had faced opposition from various quarters of the federal government: the State Department, which had sought a lead role in peacetime intelligence; the armed services, which had wanted no civilian interference in their own operations; and the Federal Bureau of Investigation (FBI), whose director J. Edgar Hoover saw a major rival and competitor and never moderated his stiff resistance during his own long tenure in office.

To a large extent, the design of the new agency followed the recommendations of William "Wild Bill" Donovan, the former head of the wartime Office of Strategic Services (OSS), which had grown to over 10,000 worldwide operatives. Above all, he had called for "the establishment for the first time in our nation's history of a foreign secret intelligence service which reported information as seen through American eyes." Stressing the importance of its independence from other government departments, Donovan further urged research and analysis to become "an integral and inseparable part of this service." Because building a modern system – never an easy matter – was more difficult in peacetime than war, Donovan urged immediate action before the OSS completely disappeared to take advantage of "its experience and know how."[1]

Fears had to be allayed that the new organization might be generally construed as an "American Gestapo." Yet this apprehension gained little traction, in part because the legislation specifically denied the agency any police, subpoena, and law-enforcement powers as well as a domestic security function. In addition, the Japanese surprise attack on Pearl Harbor in December 1941 remained a vivid memory. Had a centralized agency been in place at that time, some argued, advance warning might well have reached the president in a timely manner, thereby averting the catastrophe that occurred. Now, with ominous communist threats taking shape throughout the world, the imperative for an organization of this sort seemed all the greater.

Somewhat ironically, for the next 15 years, the CIA facilities were scattered around the nation's capital, some located in various office buildings, others in flimsy prefabricated huts on the Mall which acquired the nickname "cockroach alley." It was not until 1961 that the persistent efforts of Allen Dulles found realization and a centralized site with a seven-story concrete-and-glass headquarters building was established in nearby suburban Langley, Virginia (the next significant physical expansion, doubling the space, did not occur until 1988). The agency's initial personnel – a mixture of lawyers, journalists, and academics – were drawn primarily from Ivy League institutions and the East Coast establishment. Many, too, arrived with a background of wartime experience in the OSS. From their perspective, working at the CIA had both an idealistic and exotic appeal. Not only did they feel that their efforts, unencumbered by the ingrained bureaucratic habits of older government departments, would make a difference, but the new agency offered the possibility of working in glamorous faraway locales. The semisecret mystique of simply "working for the US government," when asked by an outsider, should not be discounted either. As might be expected, colleagues came to form closely knit relationships in this environment, socially as well as professionally, and to regard the population at large with a certain elitist disdain.

The director of the CIA held the additional title of director of central intelligence (DCI), although this designation has a far more imposing ring than was actually the case. From the outset, lacking jurisdiction in budgetary and personnel matters apart from the CIA, the DCI has been ill equipped to assert his authority over the entire foreign intelligence community within the federal government. It is also worth noting that covert action did not explicitly form part of the CIA's original mandate. The main purpose of the agency was, rather, one of collection and coordination – to bring together and evaluate, for example, information from all areas related to national security, and to perform specific tasks as requested by the newly created National Security Council.

Soon enough, however, voices could be heard urging the establishment of this additional capability. One of its most forceful advocates was James Forrestal, the secretary of defense in the Truman administration, who argued that Soviet covert operations abroad should not go unchallenged. Another was George Kennan, recently installed as the head of the powerful Policy Planning Staff, who believed that "indigenous anti-communist elements in threatened countries of the Free World" should receive clandestine support from the US government. Especially in Europe, that came to mean providing secret assistance to the non-communist left – ranging from social democratic politicians and sympathetic trade union officials to ex-communist literary intellectuals.

Through several executive directives, an arrangement was cobbled together that resulted in the Office of Policy Coordination (OPC) under Frank Wisner, a highly able former Wall Street lawyer and OSS station chief in Romania. Possessing a most unwieldy structure, the OPC received its orders from the State Department and the Department of Defense but maintained funding and personnel links to the CIA. Its head was appointed by the secretary of state, not the DCI. Still, this configuration proved no barrier to its rapid expansion, for, by 1952, the OPC could count 47 foreign stations and a staff of 2,812, not including an equally large supplemental force of contracted individuals. Those OPC officers stationed abroad – usually as second-in-command in their respective embassies – had considerable freedom of action and often the ability to initiate their own operations. Should anything go awry, a provision was officially formulated for "plausible deniability," thereby shielding the president from accusations of direct responsibility. In his subsequent memoirs, Truman wrote of his strong distaste for "peacetime cloak and dagger operations," but this recollection runs directly counter to the historical record. US covert action had its birth during his tenure in the White House, its authorization bearing his signature.

The emergence of the CIA was not just a domestic matter. The recent wartime alliance had sealed the "special relationship" between the United States and Great Britain, and it seemed almost axiomatic that this transatlantic tie would extend into the realm of postwar intelligence. The British, of course, could boast of a much longer tradition – one dating from the reign of Elizabeth I – and many considered their expertise in such matters to be unsurpassed by any other country. That was certainly the opinion of President Franklin D. Roosevelt, who had expressed high praise for their earlier performance during World War I.

An immediate priority of the British was to conclude a CIA–SIS (Secret Intelligence Service) treaty – similar to the agreements that had previously defined the wartime relationship between the OSS and the Special Operations Executive (SOE) and SIS. Indeed, that cooperation had flourished to a remarkable degree, even though the Americans were more often in the position of eager learners. It could be readily detected in the close rapport that developed between Donovan and William Stephenson, the SIS liaison to the American intelligence services, who provided entrée to the top levels of the British hierarchy, including Prime Minister Winston Churchill, King George VI, and members of the war cabinet. Daily contact was also maintained between Donovan and Colonel Stewart Menzies, the chief of SIS. Upon arriving in Britain in June 1942 as commander of the US military forces, General Dwight D. Eisenhower received a personal briefing from Churchill on Ultra, his country's successful reading of German radio traffic. It came to have immense strategic importance to Eisenhower, saving the lives of thousands of British and American soldiers and accelerating the moment of German surrender, as he acknowledged in a fulsome tribute sent to Menzies at war's end. Reflecting this close relationship, the two countries proceeded to conclude a unique agreement – not publically known until 2010 – to refrain from spying on one another and not to recruit each other's nationals without permission (with the addition of Canada, Australia, and New Zealand, this group became known as the "Five Eyes" club or alliance).

Yet, in one important respect, the CIA that began to take shape after 1947 must have caused a measure of consternation in London. One of the few lessons that the British had taken to heart from the Americans was Donovan's insistence that secret intelligence and secret operations function more effectively when placed under a single authority, not in rival entities. Accordingly, the British had merged SOE with SIS after 1945 in a manner resembling the OSS. By contrast, US covert action was only semi-attached to the CIA in the OPC – a situation that stubbornly persisted for a number of years before formal integration occurred.

Another key reversal in the partnership between the two countries involved signals intelligence (SIGINT) – the generic term for deriving information from the interception of electromagnetic waves. As Ultra had so clearly demonstrated, the British wartime cryptanalysts had held the upper hand, but with the creation of the National Security Agency (NSA) in 1952 – and the abundant resources and support that it received throughout the Eisenhower administration – it was the Americans who were to take the undisputed SIGINT lead in the Western world. If for no other reason, the severe economic doldrums experienced by postwar Britain prevented the country from making the costly high-tech investments that modern communications increasingly demanded. The huge technical apparatus at its disposal allowed the NSA, head-quartered at Fort Meade, Maryland, to attempt to collect all Soviet transmissions – ranging from every conventional radio broadcast in all the Soviet republics to every message sent to its foreign embassies to every communication involving military units on maneuver.

A further difference between the two allies came into play as well. Whereas the Americans displayed an almost single-minded focus on the

Cold War and the Soviet bloc, the British had to address an additional situation of utmost importance. Their far-flung Commonwealth found itself in a crucial transitional phase. As India edged toward independence from colonial rule, for example, officials in London expressed mounting concern about the confidentiality of secret and top-secret material sent to New Delhi, primarily because of the radicalism of the Indian High Commissioner, Krishna Menon. American anxiety about Britain's dual commitment hardly seemed ill founded. According to an internal British report in 1949, which ranked Commonwealth members according to their level of government security, only Canada could be confidently placed in the first category. A distinct divergence in viewpoint could also be detected when assessing a country such as Iran. Besides seeking to protect its major interest in the country's southern oil fields, Britain still had a proclivity to think in imperial terms, while the United States worried primarily about communist incursions in the region.

That threat, of course, emanated from the Soviet Union and particularly from its formidable security apparatus. Founded in virtual secrecy in December 1917 amidst the Bolshevik Revolution, it had become known for most citizens as the Cheka – an abbreviation of the All-Russian Extraordinary Commission for Combating Counter-Revolution and Sabotage. Its head, appointed by V. I. Lenin, was Feliks Dzerzhinsky, a deeply committed Polish revolutionary who had been repeatedly imprisoned by Tsarist authorities. Once in command of the Cheka, he had no compunctions whatsoever in carrying out a merciless campaign of arrests and executions – the so-called Red Terror – that quickly claimed thousands of lives. Aimed less at specific opposition groups and often targeting innocent individuals, it sought, above all, to create an atmosphere of widespread fear and intimidation. Strikingly, too, most of Dzerzhinsky's deputies were non-Russian as well – Latvians, Armenians, and Jews – as Lenin regarded Russians themselves as too "soft" to carry out the harsh measures that the revolution required. A workaholic like Lenin, Dzerzhinsky acquired the nickname "Iron Feliks" because of his ascetic lifestyle and exceptional powers of endurance. His characterization of his fellow Chekists – that they possessed "a warm heart, a cool head, and clean hands" – found seemingly endless repetition in the lavish propaganda later produced by the security forces.

Even before Dzerzhinsky's death in 1926, the security forces had begun to experience a series of fusions, separations, and re-subordinations that mostly reflected internal party machinations, causing the names to change accordingly. Even so, the traditional functions, unlike the fluctuating nomenclature, showed little variance over time. In 1945, the apparatus was known as the NKGB/MGB. The pivotal person was

Lavrenti Beria, who had been brought to Moscow in 1938 to direct the final phase of Stalin's purges and whose influence had expanded to an unusual degree during the war. Despite their intimate relationship – one biographer has called the fellow Georgian Stalin's alter ego[2]– Beria's accretion of power and prestige began to disturb the Soviet leader, and certain brakes were discreetly applied. By 1947, he had lost visible control of his state security and intelligence empire.

Increasingly old and suspicious, Stalin then ordered the secret creation of the Komitet Informatsii (Committee of Information, or KI) so that all collected data about the outside world – which had grown immeasurably – could be systematically verified by a single unit. Since this unusual bureaucratic reordering occurred only a few months after the creation of the CIA, some have speculated that Stalin might have been emulating the American example, but no definitive corroboration thus far exists. In fact, the KI took centralization several steps further by establishing a large umbrella organization that fused all departments dealing with foreign intelligence and clandestine operations. It soon occupied a new headquarters in the former Comintern buildings near the Agricultural Exhibit in Moscow.

Fatal friction, however, started to develop almost immediately. Two of the rival intelligence services – the First Directorate of the Soviet State Security (MGB) and the Main Intelligence Directorate of the Soviet General Staff (GRU) – preferred to bypass the KI's analytical office and go directly to Stalin with an exclusive piece of information. They then managed to regain their formal independence from the committee by the end of 1949. In addition, Foreign Minister V. M. Molotov, the first head of the committee, fell increasingly out of favor with the Soviet ruler and was replaced briefly by Andrei Vyshinsky, the notorious show trial prosecutor of the 1930s, who quickly admitted his lack of competence in such sensitive intelligence matters. The large KI thus ended in failure, although a smaller KI continued to function and lasted through the period of collective leadership.

Just as Stalin refrained from naming a successor prior to the end of his reign, so, too, a near anarchic situation had come to prevail among the party elite in the Politburo. According to Nikita Khrushchev, "The government virtually ceased to exist … . Everyone in the orchestra was playing on his own instrument anytime he felt like it, and there was no direction from the conductor."[3] Following Stalin's death in March 1953, Beria went on the offensive and sought to bring foreign intelligence, counterintelligence, police, and security services under his sway as a stepping stone toward becoming the new Soviet ruler. This rash move, however, proved to be his undoing. Faced with both real and spurious charges (such as spying for the British since the 1920s), Beria was tried by a secret court, pronounced guilty, and shot the same evening. Six presumed co-conspirators also perished as a result. Even though the leadership had compiled 40 volumes of evidence and testimony, his most heinous crimes involving the murder and repression of thousands of innocent victims went unmentioned.

In March 1954, as one of Khrushchev's chief reforms of the Stalinist system, Soviet state security saw its final reorganization as the KGB – "Committee of State Security under the Council of Ministers." Its title reflected an attempt to place it under tighter political control, as the new Soviet leader proudly announced the infusion of fresh, loyal cadres from the party and "the restoration of Leninist norms." Cuts in salaries, pensions, and benefits drove home the point even further. But a closer look shows that the post-Stalin purges of the state security organs rarely went beyond a small circle of political enemies and left the vast majority of officials untouched. In December 1957, to mark the fortieth anniversary of the founding of the Cheka, Ivan Serov, the longtime ally whom Khrushchev had appointed to head the KGB, carefully noted that "the newcomers" were laboring alongside "old experienced workers to whom the Central Committee and the party accorded their complete trust and support."[4]

Internally the new organization contained a series of chief directorates and directorates, and by the mid-1970s counted approximately 50,000 employees in Moscow alone – larger than the combined staffs of the CIA and FBI. Not only its immensity but its sheer bureaucratic complexity could hardly elude an outside observer. Most relevant in the context of the Cold War was the First Chief Directorate, which had responsibility for foreign intelligence and operated through a worldwide network of hundreds of intelligence stations or *rezidenturas*. Yet, the Second Chief Directorate, which was charged with domestic counterintelligence, also had a very significant role to play. It possessed the capacity not only to target foreign agents and émigré political and religious organizations but also to penetrate diplomatic and consular missions in the USSR and to secure recruitments among visiting businessmen and students.

Khrushchev's reforms further entailed a new orientation for the security organization. Immediately after the war, Stalin's ever hardening vision had divided the world into two hostile and irreconcilable camps – capitalist and communist – with no concessions to a middle ground. Accordingly the intelligence apparatus directed the bulk of its attention to the United States, which had just officially replaced Great Britain as the "main adversary" (*glarniy protivnik*). He no longer saw any grave danger, given the decolonization of the great European empires then underway, having begun with the termination of British rule in India in 1947.

Abandoning Stalin's strictly defined two-camp theory, his successor seized upon the emerging national liberation movements with his typically robust fervor. Khrushchev's unwavering confidence in the inherent superiority of the Soviet command economy led to thousands of Soviet investments in the Third World. The rhetoric, as well, never ceased to denounce alleged imperialist exploitation by the West – even in the postcolonial era – and to praise the struggles of oppressed peoples to gain independence. Especially among top KGB personnel – in sharp contrast to those in the Foreign Ministry – the conviction grew that the path to victory in the Cold War lay unequivocally in the Third World. As a young officer in the Latin American department later recalled, "this was the basic premise" – that the "destiny of the world confrontation between the United States and the Soviet Union, between Capitalism and Socialism, would be resolved" there.[5]

Underscoring this new emphasis was a fresh generation of KGB officers who began to appear in the late 1950s, replacing the quite dogmatic and insular group who had begun their careers immediately after World War II. Selected on the basis of their proven party loyalty, their family connections, and their physical appearance, they had studied foreign history, culture, languages, and diplomatic protocol, often at elite schools such as the Institute for International Studies in Moscow. Komsomol, the communist youth organization, served as the main reservoir of potential recruits. After joining the KGB, they received intensive training in the full range of espionage work – from the basics of coding and cryptography to the use of psychological techniques. To emphasize the seriousness of their new occupation, classmates were forbidden to divulge their actual surnames to one another. Better attired, they tended to project greater self-confidence and individuality than those found, for example, in the diplomatic service. Fears of "Zionist subversion" ran deep in the KGB, which meant that Jews were generally barred from its ranks, reversing the recruitment policy that had prevailed from the earliest days until the end of World War II.

The continuing growth of the KGB's power and prestige could likewise be seen in the new headquarters for the First Chief Directorate in Yasenevo, a heavily forested area in southwestern Moscow. Opened in 1972 to relieve the overcrowding at the traditional Lubyanka location, it borrowed its basic design from the CIA's headquarters in suburban Langley, Virginia. No cost was seemingly spared in the construction of the facility – imported materials and furniture, a sports complex and swimming pool, even an artificial lake to enhance the bucolic view from the glass-paneled offices in the main seven-story Y-shaped building. Within the KGB it became known simply as "The Forest." The exceptionally tight security featured rings of barbed wire and electronic sensors around the compound, watchtowers manned by trained personnel, and designated buses for the transportation of the thousands of secretaries and low-level workers. Top officials had their own car and driver.

To assist the KGB in its endeavors, new resources soon took shape in the so-called people's democracies of Eastern Europe. For the Russians, Germany remained the undisputed top priority as it had been ever since the days of Lenin. Immediately after the arrival of the Red Army, the Soviet Military Administration was established in the eastern sector of the divided country to oversee the nuts-and-bolts of daily occupation. Its tasks included supervising the nascent German political police (known as Kommissariat-5), as well as conducting security investigations of its own. Prior to the establishment of the German Democratic Republic (GDR) in 1949, large informer networks had been set up with the assistance of the NKVD (the Soviet People's Commissariat of Internal Affairs), and, under the guise of de-Nazification, thousands of opponents of communist political control including many Social Democrats were placed in internment camps that only recently had been in the service of the Nazis. These developments occurred in clear violation of measures adopted by the Allied Control Council, which had restricted the German police forces to the maintenance of law and order and banned any political function.

The heavy imprint of the Soviet security organs continued after the establishment of the GDR's own Ministry of State Security (MfS, or Stasi) in February 1950. Every head of a service unit had his own Soviet "instructor," and the MfS occasionally had to relinquish control of an important investigation. Moreover, all three men who came to lead the ministry – Wilhelm Zaisser, Ernst Wollweber, and Erich Mielke – had been trained by Moscow and needed Soviet approval for their appointment. Neither the GDR parliament nor the Council of Ministers exercised any oversight function in regard to the MfS; the KGB was the sole *de facto* master. As Markus Wolf, the long-serving head of the foreign intelligence branch (HVA), later noted, "The structure of our 'apparat' was an exact mirror of the Soviet model. The diction of our guidelines betrayed their translation from the Russian and laid down the main goals of our future work."[6] Even regarding athletic activities for Stasi personnel, the Soviets exported their organizational model of the Dynamo Sports Association, which had been founded by Dzerzhinsky in 1923 to promote "strength, dexterity, courage, and endurance" among members of the Cheka.

But, over time, MfS officers began to acquire a visible degree of autonomy from the "friends," as they euphemistically referred to their KGB colleagues. That meant, for example, occasionally withholding certain pieces of information even though Moscow was intent on knowing everything. The Stasi actually succeeded in establishing a degree of parity and respect that none of the other Eastern bloc services ever achieved. Accorded the status of a directorate, the KGB residency in the East Berlin district of Karlshorst became its largest installation outside of the USSR – roughly 600 workers – and gained the reputation of a favored posting, not least because of its close proximity to affluent West Berlin.

By one important measure, the East Germans easily outdistanced the Soviets. At the time of its dissolution, the Stasi could count one full-time worker for every 180 GDR citizens. The ratio in the Soviet Union for the KGB was only about 595, while other Eastern bloc states ranked even lower – 876 in Czechoslovakia and 1,574 in Poland.[7] The ubiquity of the East German security forces was further reinforced by their geographic distribution. Whereas nearly half of the employees could be found in the sprawling main headquarters complex in Berlin-Lichtenberg, the remaining personnel were posted in offices outside the capital on both the regional and county levels. In fact, the majority of informers – or unofficial collaborators (*inoffizielle Mitarbeiter*) in the language of the MfS – were recruited through the county offices.

By the early 1970s, the MfS's Foreign Intelligence Department – Hauptverwaltung Aufklärung (HVA) – had established a significant presence in the Third World. Besides providing crucial support to Moscow's own strategic program, it conveyed a sense of self-importance to a country struggling for international recognition. To the HVA's longtime head, Markus Wolf, these far-flung activities even nurtured the impression of being on the winning side of the Cold War. Among the countries receiving Stasi assistance in setting up their own security services were Cuba, Zanzibar, Tanzania, Ghana, Mozambique, Angola, and Ethiopia. In addition, guerilla fighters associated with liberation movements in Rhodesia, Namibia, and South Africa received military and intelligence training at facilities in the GDR. Following the advent of formal political contacts with the Palestinian Liberation Army in late 1972 came orders for the HVA to form an intelligence link with Yasser Arafat's group – a move strongly backed by Moscow. In exchange – according to Wolf – the PLO agreed to end terrorist attacks in Europe.

The high priority that the Soviets placed on replicating their own security forces found expression in other Eastern bloc states as well, the only exceptions being Yugoslavia and Albania, where no KGB advisors were present. In Hungary, by the end of 1945, hundreds of full-time officers already worked for the state security department – the Államvédelmi Osztály (AVO) – even before any attempts were made to restore the Danube bridges in Budapest destroyed during the war. Strikingly, too, the AVO established its headquarters at 60 Andrássy Street, already notorious as the address of the Hungarian fascist police during the final brutal phase of the war, and reported directly to the party leadership, blatantly ignoring the provisional coalition government. Prior to the Hungarian Revolution of 1956, the AVO had changed its name to the Államvédelmi Hatosag (State Security Authority, or AVH), but to the thousands of anti-government protesters, this alteration was merely cosmetic, and deadly clashes resulted. Czechoslovakia also quickly saw the establishment of its own monolithic political police – the Státni Bezpecnost (State Security, or StB) – whose recruits were predominantly young blue-collar workers with scant education. Initially targeting non-communist political parties and the Catholic church, particularly in Slovakia, it shifted its focus in the mid-1950s to the surveillance of the workplace and defectors. The StB's ranks, however, suffered severely from the purges following the Prague Spring in 1968 – nearly three-quarters of the command was eliminated by the "normalization" regime – and never fully recovered its morale. Its headquarters was located in a drab concrete-and-glass building not far from Wenceslas Square.

The tightest relationship of all existed with the Bulgarian service – Durzhavna Sigurnost (State Security, or DS) – seen in many quarters as a mere extension of the KGB headed by the Russian station chief in Sofia. It displayed a particular ruthlessness in tracking down émigré critics of the regime of Tudor Zhivkov. The "Bulgarian umbrella" acquired widespread notoriety after one was used in London in 1978 to discharge small poisonous pellets containing ricin into Georgi Markov, a dissident journalist employed by the BBC World Service and considered to be a traitor for siding with the enemy. In Romania – after Soviet troops entered Bucharest in August 1945 – NKVD operatives took over the pre-communist Siguranta and supervised the formation of the Directia Generala a Securitatii Poporului, which commonly became known as the Securitate. By 1951, it contained a separate directorate for foreign intelligence. Soviet advisors were withdrawn in 1964, creating a unique situation among the Eastern bloc services, even though collaboration with the KGB continued on a regular basis.

Poland's secret police – originally the Urzad Bezpieczenstwa and then, after 1956, the Sluzba Bezpieczenstw (SB) – proved rather problematic and required sensitive handling. While its numbers rapidly escalated from some 2,500 in December 1944 to 23,700 less than a year later – and most were the children of Polish workers and peasants – the new recruits were conspicuously lacking in formal education and motivated more by careerism than communist ideology. One senior KGB officer referred to his Polish colleagues as "a wild and carefree bunch," effective in penetrating native circles abroad and acquiring valuable military and technological information but seemingly oblivious to the activities of subversive groups in their own backyard.[8] MfS chief Erich Mielke likewise expressed his own pointed reservations when having to conduct a joint operation with the SB.

To the west, in the Federal Republic of Germany, the emergence of an organized foreign intelligence capability came about largely through the efforts of Reinhard Gehlen. Descended from a family of career military officers, he had achieved distinction in World War II as the head of Fremde Heere Ost (Foreign Armies East, or FHO), the German General Staff's intelligence unit stationed on the Eastern front. His realistic reports on Germany's deteriorating position in the face of the Red Army's advance led to his dismissal in April 1945. Yet, he was convinced that his country would have a significant role to play in the near future given the artificiality of the Allied alliance. Anticipating the new struggle that was about to surface in the Cold War, Gehlen sought to insure a position for himself by having copies of the comprehensive FHO archives placed in 50 sealed drums and buried near Bad Reichenhall in Bavaria, a region that he knew would come under US occupation.

Because the Americans possessed so little information on the Soviet Union at that point, it was not difficult for Gehlen, while technically liable for war crimes prosecution, to persuade authorities of his usefulness and have his unit reconstituted an operational branch of US Army intelligence (code name RUSTY). He additionally offered the prospect of an intelligence network in Eastern Europe, since some FHO agents had been left behind during the retreat of the Wehrmacht. In his subsequent memoirs, Gehlen stressed to his German critics that he was working "with" and not "for" the Americans and that no operation was ever undertaken contrary to Germany's self-interest.

Organisation Gehlen (OG), or simply Org Gehlen as it was commonly known, began the recruitment of personnel in fall 1946 and soon established a permanent base in Pullach outside Munich, where extensive facilities within the compound made the staff and families generally independent of the outside world. Among those joining the OG were former diplomats, civil servants, and military officers, who saw it as a transitional home prior to the founding of the Bundeswehr. With the creation of the CIA the following year, serious questions were raised about the OG's continued operation, but a two-month investigation concluded that no other viable alternative in Germany existed. Although the CIA assumed official control of the OG in July 1949 (code name ZIPPER), Gehlen resisted inquiries regarding its structure and sources as best he could.

His chief aim was the adoption of the OG as the foreign intelligence service for the young Federal Republic. After outmaneuvering two competitors and weathering some heated political debate, Gehlen saw his wish fulfilled with the announcement of the Bundesnachrichtendienst (Federal Intelligence Service, or BND) in April 1956. While formally attached to the Chancellor's Office, it had few oversight mechanisms, and Gehlen retained the same freedom of action that he had enjoyed under the Americans. His new title of president rather than general director seemed mostly a formality, as the organization evinced little structural change, and the prime operational focus continued to be the GDR. Even though a few attempts were made to depict Gehlen as an unrepentant Nazi, primarily in the British press, he maintained generally cordial relations with West German journalists and even had a few on the BND payroll. His aloofness and cultivated aura of mystery (alias Dr. Schneider) worked to his advantage.

Not until Gehlen's departure in 1968 did the BND make far-reaching alterations in its *modus operandi*. Some significant problems had come to light beforehand, notably the inadequate vetting procedures that had permitted a seasoned KGB agent, Heinz Felfe, to become chief of the counterintelligence section for the Soviet Union. Even though the BND's entire network in Eastern Europe had been destroyed as a result, Gehlen managed to survive in office. With the accession of Gerhard Wessel – a close associate dating from the FHO – all domestic surveillance ended and became the exclusive preserve of the internal security agency, the Bundesamt für Verfassungsschutz (Federal Office for the Protection of the Constitution, or BfV). In addition, the extensive use of ex-Nazis was curtailed, a new signals intelligence program was inaugurated, and the organization became less secretive and recast more in the mold of a traditional civil service. These reforms extended to the BND's mission as well. Wessel expanded contacts with other friendly secret service organizations and shifted the almost exclusive focus on Eastern Europe, especially the GDR, to the world at large.

Neighboring France, as it emerged from the war, faced a bewildering historical legacy in attempting to construct a new foreign intelligence service. The disarray was acute, particularly for a state that prized centralization and rationalization to such a high degree and that also had to accept a much diminished and uncertain role in world affairs. Overcoming the sheer fragmentation formed the first order of business. In

November 1944, the Direction Générale des Service Spéciaux – the Free French organization which had fused three different groups the previous year – became the Direction Générale des Études et Recherches with responsibility for collecting information from abroad. Its numbers immediately swelled to 10,000 officers and agents – many of dubious character; but a reorganization conducted by André Dewarin – known during the war as Colonel Passy, the able intelligence chief of Charles de Gaulle – eliminated the most unsavory elements and reduced its size to roughly 1,500 persons, mostly soldiers. Renamed the Service de Documentation Extérieure et de Contre-espionage (SDECE) in January 1946, it initially reported to the War Ministry but, owing to a scandal, was later placed under the direct authority of the prime minister. A further change in nomenclature occurred in 1981 when it became the Direction Générale de la Sécurité Extérieure (DGSE).

Three separate intelligence organizations could be found in the Interior Ministry. Yet, under the efficient and rigorous leadership of Roger Wybot, the Direction de la Surveillance du Territoire (DST) quickly gained the dominant position over its competitors in the area of domestic security. But that ascendancy did not preclude clashes with the SDECE, which resented the transfer of some of the army's counter-intelligence functions to the DST. Intense personal rivalries – frequently within the same organization – only added to the turf battles. They included soldiers pitted against civilians, former Vichy officials against those who had chosen exile in London, and Gaullist loyalists against traditional socialists.

Most problematic of all, however, were the conspiratorial aspirations of the Parti communiste français (French Communist Party, or PCF). Attempting to capitalize on its prominent role in the French Resistance, its leaders had planned to seize power through a "national insurrection" in 1944, but too many factors made it seem an unadvisable move at the time. Rather, a new tactic of infiltrating the mighty state administration was adopted. Since they were considered the chief impediments to a communist takeover of the country, the army, the police, and the secret services had top priority. Moscow lent its strong support, as the KGB residency in Paris eventually ran more agents than any of its other stations in Western Europe for most of the Cold War. By 1953 at least four officials in the SDECE and one in the DST were deemed valuable assets.

The fact that the PCF had the support of one quarter of the population and sat in the government until 1947 gave it additional opportunities as well. With control of important portfolios such as Labor, Air, and Industry, it could appoint either fellow members or sympathizers to influential positions. The SDECE knew all too well that any information conveyed to the government would be promptly compromised. One ranking member, Philippe Thyraud de Vojoli, later recalled that as long as communist ministers existed in the cabinet, it was "almost impossible" for his organization "to carry out any activity ... . As a rule, everyone pretended to be busy, with the aim of being as inefficient as possible."[9] If one of its members ever came under the threat of an outside investigation, the PCF could provide a thick layer of insulation by mounting a vociferous press campaign or by publishing fragments of confidential documents so as to disqualify the case from ever reaching the courts.

To a large extent, the SDECE found itself isolated both at home and abroad. It attracted strident domestic critics with the PCF in the forefront, likening the organization to the Gestapo and labeling it a state within a state. Across the channel, mistrust of the French had deep roots in British intelligence along with the population at large. Still chagrined at France's passive surrender to Germany in 1940, officials now felt dismayed by the strong communist presence in the upper levels of the government and state administration. As negotiations began to shape the future North Atlantic Treaty Organization (NATO), the British expressly warned the Americans of the dangers of sharing sensitive data with the French. The first head of the CIA, Admiral Roscoe H. Hillenkoeter, who had previously served as US naval attaché in Paris, showed no hesitation in stating his own strong reservations regarding the issue of French security.

At the same time, the CIA viewed France as a critical battleground that could not be simply ignored. In addition to the open support authorized by the Marshall Plan – France was the second largest recipient of US assistance after Britain – so-called "unvouchered funds" were enthusiastically urged by the American Federation of Labor. This clandestine aid sought to establish for workers an independent alternative to the Soviet-dominated World Federation of Trade Unions.

When Israel finally achieved the status of statehood in May 1948, it confronted the task of completely restructuring its intelligence capacity as expeditiously as possible. Chairing a meeting six weeks later was Isser Be'eri, the head of the National Information Service, or SHAI, the intelligence arm of the Haganah which was formed in 1940 at the onset of World War II and continued to operate during the bitter struggles of the British Mandate's final years. Be'eri used the occasion to announce the decision of the country's first prime minister, David Ben-Gurion, to dismantle SHAI and distribute its functions among several separate agencies. In addition to the General Staff's intelligence service, Sherut ha'Modi'in, two other bodies came into existence: one was the innocuously named Political Department within the foreign ministry, the other the General Security Service, a domestic unit commonly known by its Hebrew acronyms Shabak or Shin Bet.

This arrangement, however, turned out to be short-lived. A slender strip of land surrounded by hostile neighbors, Israel could ill afford to perpetuate the hazily defined jurisdictions and the clash of egos that was occurring at nearly every level. The most serious dispute cast the defense ministry against the foreign ministry, each claiming the right to operate abroad. Although a compromise was engineered by Reuven Shiloah, the head of the Coordinating Committee of the Intelligence Services, it, too, provided a less than satisfactory solution and led to a more far-reaching structural change in March 1951. According to a directive issued by Ben-Gurion, the Political Department was abolished as an entity with many of its members transferred to a new more centralized civilian organization, the Ha Mossad le Teum or Institute for Coordination. Ten years later, it received its present-day designation, Ha-Mossad le Modin ule-Tafkadim Meyuhadim or Institute for Intelligence and Special Tasks.

The new Mossad became attached to the prime minister's office and directly responsible to Ben-Gurion, who then appointed Shiloah as its first director. Although it began to acquire more functions in the following years – such as the handling of Israeli spies abroad – its original task consisted primarily of foreign intelligence-gathering with no active role in covert activities. Shiloah especially sought contact with ethnic and religious groups since they formed a bulwark against a communist takeover of the country. Any group feeling the discrimination of Muslim majorities – whether the Druze in Syria, the Kurds in Iraq, the Maronites in Lebanon, or the Christians in southern Sudan – were considered potential allies as well. Shiloah's brief tenure, however, ended in September 1952 following a disastrous operation in Iraq and the revelation of an important Egyptian double agent stationed in Rome.

Yet, before his departure, confidential contacts between the Mossad and the CIA had been established at his urging. Shiloah's overriding aim was to abandon Israel's pro-Soviet stance and anchor the country in the Western alliance. At first, the Americans appeared highly skeptical, wary of a self-professed socialist state rooted in the kibbutzim and also fearful of damaging delicate relations with nearby Arab states. But the proposal put forth by both Shiloah and Ben-Gurion – that Israel could supply vital up-to-date information about the USSR and Eastern Europe that the CIA so sorely lacked – was a persuasive one to DCI Walter Bedell Smith and his assistant, Allen Dulles. Under the rubric of Operation BALSAM, this information was obtained from the security personnel's thorough interrogation of newly arrived immigrants from behind the Iron Curtain and covered a wide range of topics that they knew firsthand from their daily lives. As part of the agreement, Israel and the United States further agreed not to spy on one another. Even though the Americans were the prime beneficiary of this budding relationship, the Mossad received training and state-of-the-art equipment in return. In 1956, the CIA's respect for the Israeli service soared to new heights when a Mossad liaison officer managed to convey to his American counterpart the full text of Khrushchev's secret speech denouncing Stalin.

Isser Harel, the initial director of Shin Bet (and the only person ever to serve in both capacities), became Shiloah's successor and left a major mark on the service. A top priority was the placement of spies in every Arab capital, who then provided a steady stream of valuable information to Mossad headquarters in Tel Aviv. He also facilitated the safe departure of 80,000 Moroccan Jews to Israel after French colonial rule ended in 1956. Yet the wily Israeli spymaster, known only as Ha'Memuneh or "the boss," became most celebrated for a quite different endeavor. After assembling a special Nazi-hunting unit in the Mossad, he spearheaded the daring operation that captured Adolf Eichmann in Buenos Aires, Argentina, in May 1960 and brought him back to Jerusalem to be tried for his complicity in the Final Solution. Remarkably, too, Harel's team managed Eichmann's abduction relying solely on HUMINT with the exception of a rotating license plate installed on one of their automobiles. *The House on Garibaldi Street* – an authoritative best-selling account of this exploit written by Harel at Ben-Gurion's request – appeared after his retirement from active service.

At the same time, Harel took the controversial step of cementing a clandestine relationship with West Germany's BND in 1957 – eight years prior to the establishment of diplomatic ties between the two countries. Despite the large number of former Third Reich officials engaged by the BND, Harel believed that his country's security requirements outweighed any emotional or moralistic considerations. Reinhard Gehlen, who had initiated the contact, granted the Israelis operational freedom on West German soil as well as access to excerpts from his agency's daily briefings to the Chancellor's Office. In return, BND officers became frequent visitors to Tel Aviv and privy to many of the Russian and East European immigrant debriefings. Some US intelligence officials harbored the suspicion that incriminating evidence about ex-Nazis in the West German government was being purposely suppressed by the Mossad in exchange for preferential treatment by the BND.

Beginning in 1963, the Mossad underwent a series of significant changes under Harel's successor, Meir Amit. Of contrasting temperament and accustomed to military command, he sought to modernize the service and refocus on its primary task of collecting military and political data on the Arab states, particularly Israel's immediate neighbors known as the "inner circle." Women received expanded opportunities on the administrative level, and a more corporate style of management came to prevail, symbolized by moving Mossad headquarters to a downtown office building in Tel Aviv. Still one final retributive action against Nazi war criminals took place at Amit's direction. Believing that another kidnapping and trial would not have the same impact upon world opinion, he decided that the simpler and more effective course was to murder the targeted person outright – in this case, Herbert Cukurs, a well-known Latvian aviator who had acquired the title of the "butcher of Riga." Above all, it would serve as a signal to West European governments not to halt their own pursuit and prosecution of these war criminals. The deed was accomplished in May 1965 by luring Cukurs from his residence in Brazil to a Mossad safe house in Montevideo, Uruguay. A note attached to his chest was signed by "those who would never forget."

The foundation of the intelligence apparatus of the People's Republic of China (PRC) predates the country's emergence after the communist conquest of the Chinese mainland in 1949. The dominant figure was Kang Sheng, the son of a wealthy landowning family who chose the path of communist activism in 1924 while a student in Shanghai. Maintaining a close association with the NKVD – and absorbing firsthand the finer techniques of Stalin's purges – he later spent four years in Moscow completing his political education before becoming a key member of Mao Zedong's inner circle. In 1938, Kang's position solidified with his appointment as head of the new Social Affairs Department. Designed to bring three previous agencies into a single entity, it had far-reaching powers and rapidly evolved into a ruthless instrument under Kang's direction, reinforced by his additional title as head of military intelligence. In the tense atmosphere of extreme instability and shifting personal allegiances, his main targets included the rival Kuomintang and the Japanese special service units found throughout the country.

In 1945, Kang lost both of his official posts and was assigned other responsibilities, mostly on the local level. Nevertheless, his undeniable influence on intelligence and security matters continued to be felt in the next decades, not only owing to his various protégés but also through the harsh methods and institutions that bear his signature. Kang's name also became closely associated with the advent of the Cultural Revolution, as he set into motion a vast self-perpetuating system of persecution that singled out what he called "renegades," "enemy agents," and "traitors."

A new apparatus formed in October 1949 – the Ministry of Public Security – assumed many of the functions of the Social Affairs Department and made internal surveillance its primary focus, while the latter continued to collect intelligence from abroad. Additional reorganizations followed, the most significant occurring in June 1983 with the establishment of the Guoanbu (Ministry of State Security, or MSS) – the country's preeminent civilian intelligence agency. In the context of the Cold War, it is important to note that the PRC displayed much less interest in the global balance of forces than those nations with far-flung military commitments such as the United States and the USSR. Consequently, its intelligence organizations concentrated on issues that primarily affected the country's internal and regional stability – notably, Taiwan and Tibet – as well as the procurement of advanced scientific and technological data.

Further differences surfaced as well. For overseas operations, the MSS embraced the practice of enlisting large numbers of ethnic Chinese living or traveling outside the country rather than relying on fewer spies with access to more confidential sources. Likewise, at sharp variance with Western and Soviet procedure, one finds little evidence of the conventional techniques of Cold War espionage such as clandestine meetings, dead drops, and aerial reconnaissance. Much preferred is a more casual exploitation of personal and professional contacts and the gradual accumulation of desired information. Lastly – to the considerable frustration of Western counterintelligence – defections from the communist Chinese services have occurred relatively seldom, thus making knowledge of their internal dynamics all the more difficult to fathom.

Although the Japanese are known for their longstanding affinity for intelligence work, its actual governmental institutionalization did not begin until the 1930s and was designed primarily to secure the country's strategic position in Asia and the Pacific. Following Japan's defeat in World War II, intelligence operatives found themselves thoroughly discredited, along with members of the military, and placed under the supervision of the Western occupation forces. Only slowly did various governmental bodies start to reappear. The clearest product of the Cold War was the Public Security Investigative Agency (*koanchosa-cho*, or PSIA), established in 1952 with the end of the occupation. Eventually becoming the country's largest civilian intelligence agency, it had the task of monitoring the activities of the Japanese Communist Party, later broadened to include a variety of right-wing groups and foreign subversives. While its mandate might be compared to the US's FBI or Great

Britain's MI5, the PSIA, however, lacks the police power of arrest and compulsory investigations.

Also noteworthy is the Cabinet Intelligence Research Office (*naikaku joho chosa-shitsu*), one of six divisions of the Cabinet Secretariat within the prime minister's office. While resembling the CIA in some respects, its diminutive size and lack of resources restricted its influence considerably. During the Cold War, the country's military intelligence – focused primarily on SIGINT – was conducted by a number of units spread throughout the defense establishment. Indeed, one of the prime characteristics of postwar Japanese intelligence stemmed from its diffuse nature. The collection and analysis of most foreign intelligence occurred within the larger bureaucracies of the police, the foreign ministry, and the trade and industry ministry. A significant Japanese covert action capability, it appears, never materialized.

Notes

1 Cited by Thomas F. Troy, *Donovan and the CIA: A History of the Establishment of the Central Intelligence Agency* (Frederick, MD: University Publications of America, 1981), 290.
2 Amy W. Knight, *Beria: Stalin's First Lieutenant* (Princeton, NJ: Princeton University Press, 1993), 7.
3 Strobe Talbot (Ed.), *Khrushchev Remembers* (Boston, MA: Little, Brown, 1970), 297.
4 Cited by Amy W. Knight, *The KGB: Police and Politics in the Soviet Union* (Boston, MA: Allen & Unwin, 1988), 52.
5 Cited by Christopher Andrew and Vasili Mitrokhin, *The World was Going Our Way: The KGB and the Battle for the Third World* (New York, NY: Basic Books, 2005), 10.
6 Markus Wolf (with Anne McElvoy), *Man Without a Face: The Autobiography of Communism's Greatest Spymaster* (New York, NY: Times Books, 1997), 46.
7 Jens Gieseke, *Die hauptamtlichen Mitarbeiter der Staatssicherheit: Personalstruktur und Lebenswelt 1950–1989/90* (Berlin: Ch. Links Verlag, 2000), 538.
8 Oleg Kalugin with Fen Montaigne, *The First Directorate: My 32 Years in Intelligence and Espionage Against the West* (New York, NY: St. Martin's Press, 1994), 189.
9 Cited by Douglas Porch, *The French Secret Services: From the Dreyfus Affair to the Gulf War* (New York, NY: Farrar, Straus and Giroux, 1995), 280.

3   The Early Years

The first strong indication of postwar Soviet espionage operations in North America occurred in Canada. On September 5, 1945, Igor Gouzenko, a young GRU cipher clerk, simply left the military intelligence offices of the Soviet legation in Ottawa with more than 100 highly classified documents strapped to his waist and stuffed in his pockets. Anxious to remain in Canada with his family after learning of his imminent recall to Moscow, he quickly discovered his most unwelcome presence in the host country. Neither the *Ottawa Journal* nor the Justice Ministry displayed any interest in Gouzenko's story, while the Canadian prime minister, Mackenzie King, who initially questioned the Russian's emotional stability, preferred to avoid any action that could possibly arouse the displeasure of the USSR. Only when four officials from the Soviet legation brazenly broke into Gouzenko's apartment did the Canadian government decide to grant asylum and provide a secure residence – all under the blanket of strictest secrecy until American journalist Drew Pearson broke the story on February 3, 1946.

Within a short period, investigators uncovered the existence of a major Canadian spy ring that had penetrated parliament and the civil service, even air force intelligence. Besides implicating several Americans, Gouzenko's information led, most importantly, to the arrest and confession of the British nuclear scientist Alan Nun May, the first of the atom bomb spies to be unmasked. Whatever misgivings some Canadians voiced regarding the legal propriety of the investigations and subsequent trials, the Gouzenko affair gave intelligence professionals in the West more than a rude jolt as to the breadth and depth of covert Soviet operations.

In the United States – only a few months earlier – the FBI had arrested six persons connected with the pro-communist magazine *Amerasia* for having stolen a top-secret report of the OSS discussing British policy in Asia. Yet, despite the incriminating evidence obtained by American investigators, it could not overcome the legal hurdles then in place, and the first major prosecution of the emerging Cold War came to naught – much to the anger of J. Edgar Hoover. It was the subsequent revelations of Elizabeth Bentley that was to mark a major turning point in the history of postwar espionage. A graduate of Vassar College who had drifted into the communist orbit during the Great Depression, she used her foreign language skills to obtain a position at the pro-Fascist Italian Library of Information in New York, where her career as a Soviet spy began. The relationship with her Russian handler, Jacob Golos – a senior party officer – developed into a romantic liaison, as she (code name CLEVER GIRL) was increasingly entrusted with the management of his extensive North American spy network. His death of a heart attack in 1943 gave her direct control of the Silvermaster and Perlo groups, which had heavily penetrated the Washington, DC, establishment.

Nonetheless, the KGB looked askance at the seemingly amateurish methods that Bentley and Golos had employed – individual agents, for example, needed to be more isolated from one another in smaller cells – and gradually relieved her of her responsibilities. By 1945, feeling personally and professionally bereft, Bentley, who also feared FBI surveillance, made a dramatic preemptive move by deciding to divulge to the agency everything that she knew – ultimately, the names of scores of sources working in various branches of the US government as well as KGB officers of her acquaintance. This long list of the former officials ranged from Harry Magdoff in the Department of Commerce and Abram Glasser in the Department of Justice to Lauchlin Currie and Laurence Duggan in the Department of State.

For the Soviet Union, Bentley's defection had a devastating impact. It signaled the immediate cessation of nearly all its American operations and the deactivation of its agents. The fact that long-term Soviet intelligence operations had only begun to recover from the thoroughgoing purges of Joseph Stalin prior to World War II only added to the acute sense of loss. A memorandum prepared in 1948 by Anatoly Gorsky, the KGB head of station in Washington, bore the stark title "Collapses in the United States."[1] He even contemplated various scenarios that would bring about her "physical liquidation" but was overruled by Moscow. One measure of compensation, however, was provided by the British mole Kim Philby, whose inside information allowed Soviet authorities to issue a timely warning to their operatives and thereby thwart the FBI's attempt to gather direct evidence of espionage committed by those named by Bentley. That meant that of the dozens of government officials on her list, only three low-level prosecutions resulted, none of them explicitly involving charges of espionage.

For the United States – and the FBI in particular – a new era was about to commence. Although key Soviet officials such as Walter Krivitsky of the GRU had fled to the West during the 1930s, their revelations of Stalin's hostile intentions had sounded only faint warning bells. By contrast, the FBI now established a special division and struggled to gain an expertise in matters quite removed from such traditional jurisdictions as kidnapping and illegal interstate commerce. Still, as former FBI agent Robert Lamphere later noted, working with Soviet espionage cases initially constituted an unfulfilling "Siberian" assignment, to be avoided if possible.[2] Only in gradual stages did his own awareness of the gravity of the situation begin to take shape as a special agent in the field.

Bentley herself moved to the public stage, first giving factual testimony before the US Congress in 1948, then appearing on national radio and speaking to numerous civic groups, and lastly writing a popular, somewhat embellished autobiography. Too often it is forgotten that she succeeded in convincing many Americans of the coordinated assault being waged on the independence of their government – as opposed to a series of random instances – and in spurring the Truman administration and Congress to institute internal government security programs. By the same token, Bentley did not lack numerous critics, who derisively employed the journalistic catch phrase, "the blonde spy queen" (despite her brown hair and ordinary appearance) and depicted her as a neurotic alcoholic. Her clear vindication finally came after the end of the Cold War and the release of the Venona decryptions in 1992. What had appeared to her detractors as an episode of blatant anti-Communist hysteria turned out to be a factually grounded exposé of widespread Soviet penetration.

Bentley's congressional testimony brought another central figure of the early Cold War to the fore. Whittaker Chambers, the product of a dysfunctional Long Island family, had joined the Communist Party USA (CPUSA) in the early 1920s, worked in various capacities before going "underground" ten years later, and finally broke with the party in 1938, disillusioned by Stalin's purges as well as by the duplicitous Soviet role in the Spanish Civil War. His attempts to alert the wartime Roosevelt administration and the FBI about a highly placed communist spy ring in the government ended in frustration, despite meeting with Assistant Secretary of State A. A. Berle, Jr., the president's intelligence liaison. He then turned his formidable literary talents to journalism, becoming, in the words of editor-in-chief Henry R. Luce, "the best writer that *Time* ever employed." When Chambers received a subpoena to appear before the House Committee on Un-American Activities in

August 1948, his inclination at that point was to remain close mouthed, preferring to channel his anti-communist convictions into the realm of history and ideas and, unlike Bentley, not to start naming names.

Only haltingly – and against his own instincts – did he reveal his former role as a Soviet spy and, above all, implicate his close friend Alger Hiss. He responded by challenging Chambers to repeat his charges outside the legally protected confines of a congressional hearing room. After Chambers repeated the accusation on nationwide radio, Hiss filed a slander suit, which then caused Chambers to produce long-hidden copies of classified government documents, some typed on Hiss's machine, others copied in his own hand. These so-called "Baltimore documents" dating from 1938 had been purposely retained by Chambers as insurance against reprisals from the party and were shortly supplemented by the so-called "pumpkin papers" – several strips of microfilm that had been concealed on his Maryland farm. Because the ten-year statute of limitations on espionage had lapsed, the Justice Department indicted Hiss on two counts of perjury.

The courtroom battles that ensued between the two men riveted – and divided – the country in a manner not unlike the earlier Dreyfus Affair in France. At first glance, the protagonists appeared conspicuously ill matched. Hiss's prestigious résumé could boast of a Supreme Court clerkship under Oliver Wendell Holmes, a key advisory position to President Franklin Roosevelt at the Yalta Conference, an important role in designing the newly created United Nations, and currently the presidency of the Carnegie Endowment for International Peace. Elegant in appearance and well-connected socially, he also had the support of leading figures of the Washington establishment, while Chambers – overweight, somewhat disheveled, and speaking in a barely audible monotone – seemed to lack credibility from the outset.

The main strategy of Hiss's defense team was to portray Chambers as a misfit, claiming that he suffered from a mental disease, which had led him to engage in "pathological lying" and commit "psychopathic" acts. Hiss, by contrast, was "an honest and maligned and falsely accused gentleman" whose word should not be doubted. A string of eminent witnesses including two serving Supreme Court justices also appeared on Hiss's behalf. Although the first jury deadlocked 8–4 against Hiss, a second, somewhat longer trial upheld the version of events presented by the prosecution. Particularly important was the testimony of Hede Massing, likewise a defector from the Communist Party in the late 1930s, who provided the jury with a second eyewitness description of Hiss's espionage, as well as the crucial Woodstock typewriter, which had belonged to the Hiss family and whose typeface matched the Baltimore documents. On January 25, 1950, the presiding judge gave Hiss a five-year prison sentence.

When released three years and eight months later, the former spy showed no signs of contrition whatsoever. On the contrary, he proceeded to embark on a well-honed campaign to prove his innocence and thereby restore his reputation. Whereas his two stiffly written autobiographical accounts did little to advance his cause, a personal encounter with Hiss would likely have had precisely the opposite effect. His air of apparent serenity and his gracious manner, if not wholly persuasive, at least aroused strong feelings of ambiguity about the case. From his perspective, he had the satisfaction of having fulfilled the strict commandment for Soviet agents never to reveal their dual identity regardless of the circumstances. Increasingly, though, Hiss's small band of partisans found their case weakened by new evidence, notably the release of the Venona decryptions in which he appears under the code name ALES. A broad historical consensus now regards his Soviet espionage career as an established fact. Although still a polarizing presence until his death in 1961, Chambers managed to write a powerful and best-selling autobiography simply entitled *Witness*. For later generations, as well, it provided a unique insight into the communist underground during the 1930s and helped shape many attitudes about the deeper philosophical premises of the Cold War struggle.

Coming on the heels of the Hiss trials was the rapid rise and fall of Joseph McCarthy. On February 9, 1950, in Wheeling, West Virginia, the junior senator from Wisconsin delivered his now infamous speech charging the State Department with harboring more than 200 communists. His skillful demagoguery seemed to mask the elastic numbers that he continually cited. With the appointment of Allen Dulles as DCI three years later, he quickly turned his sights on the CIA – "the worst situation" of all in his words. Threatening the first major congressional investigation of the agency, he told his colleagues: "I have roughly a hundred pages of documentation covering incompetence, inefficiency, waste and Communist infiltration in the CIA, which I am holding in the hope that a committee will be established so that I can turn the information over to it."[3]

Yet, unlike other Washington institutions, the CIA was a secret agency operating under a presidential umbrella and hence better equipped to weather the storm. McCarthy initially targeted a young analyst, William P. Bundy, hoping to use him as a wedge to stage a full-scale assault. Standing his ground, Dulles, with President Dwight D. Eisenhower's concurrence, resisted the request that Bundy appear before McCarthy's Senate Permanent Subcommittee on Investigations. Furthermore, he told a group of 600 senior officers that no one from the agency would be allowed to testify and that anyone approaching McCarthy and his associates without his permission would be subject to immediate dismissal. Dulles then authorized a number of preemptive security measures in order to stay several steps ahead of McCarthy. Significantly, too, as a spycatcher, the senator had an abysmal record, no doubt a consequence of his less than nuanced understanding of both communism and espionage. Despite the massive Soviet penetration of the federal government that had occurred, none of the persons that McCarthy recklessly named while in the limelight was ever documented as having been a foreign agent.

On the other side of the Atlantic, Britain's largest spy scandal had begun to unfold. Its roots lay in the mid-1930s, specifically in the ingenious recruiting efforts of Arnold Deutsch (code name OTTO) at Cambridge University. There the Austrian-born communist (with ties to the Soviet NKVD) had singled out young radical students who had potentially influential careers ahead of them, tactfully secured their agreement to work undercover, and then provided them with a fresh non-communist identity. Soon enough, his method paid rich dividends, for the Five, as they were initially known at the Center (or KGB headquarters), came to occupy important diplomatic and intelligence postings.[4] The prominent art historian Anthony Blunt (code name JOHNSON), who reassumed the directorship of the prestigious Courtauld Institute after 1945 and also became the surveyor of the queen's pictures, had used his wartime posting in the Security Service to betray every confidential item that passed across his desk. Despite a confession in exchange for immunity from prosecution in 1964, it was not until 15 years later that his treachery became publicly known, and Prime Minister Margaret Thatcher stripped him of his knighthood.

The subversive activities of the remaining four continued unabated into the early Cold War. Guy Burgess (code names HICKS and PAUL) – known increasingly for his flamboyant and dissolute lifestyle but still considered valuable by the Center as a prodigious supplier of classified documents – worked in the Far Eastern Department of the Foreign Office prior to his arrival in Washington, DC, in 1950 as second secretary in the British embassy. Donald Maclean (code name HOMER) occupied an even more advantageous diplomatic perch for conveying high-grade intelligence to Moscow. In 1947, he became joint secretary of the Combined Policy Committee, which coordinated Anglo-American-Canadian nuclear policy. A colleague of Maclean concluded that the material he passed on greatly strengthened the Chinese and North Korean negotiating and strategic positions with the advent of the Korean War.

Yet, upon learning that the Venona decrypts contained several references to a HOMER based in Washington and the list of suspects was narrowing, Moscow emphatically urged – and facilitated – the defection of both Burgess and Maclean to the Soviet Union in May 1951, initially against their own will. Allotted a small pension, Burgess led an idle life with no formal responsibilities, while Maclean took Soviet citizenship under a new name, taught for a while at a pedagogical institute, and was joined several years later by his wife and three children. A third member, John Cairncross (code names MOLIÈRE and LISZT), who had returned to the UK Treasury after the war and oversaw expenditures on defense research, also came under suspicion. Interrogated by MI5, he admitted conveying information to the Russians, denied being a spy, but resigned from his government post and chose to live abroad. Only in 1990 did the public learn of Cairncross's espionage. He again rejected the charge, contrary to the assertions of his former case officer, Yuri Modin, who rated him as one of the KGB's most valued British informants.

Easily the most famous of the Five was Harold Adrian Russell Philby (code name STANLEY), even though his career developed at a slower pace than the other four. Born in the Punjab and nicknamed "Kim" after the hero of the Rudyard Kipling novel, he was the son of an eccentric British civil servant and celebrated Arabist. By the time that Philby completed his education at Cambridge in June 1933, he knew that the remainder of his life "must be devoted to Communism." His first important Soviet espionage assignment involved the Spanish Civil War, where he posed as a reporter for *The Times* covering the forces assembled by General Francisco Franco. Following the outbreak of World War II, Philby succeeded in joining one of the British intelligence services – the newly created Special Operations Executive designed to conduct subversive warfare on the continent. Soon thereafter, he was offered a position as a counterintelligence expert in the Iberian subsection of the SIS.

In the postwar period – as the chief of station in Istanbul from 1947 to 1949 – Philby assisted Soviet deception operations by betraying agents who crossed the borders into the USSR as well as their contacts inside the country. His next assignment as the SIS liaison officer in Washington, DC – comparable in status to that of an ambassador – gave him significantly expanded opportunities. Not only did he have regular briefings from both the FBI and the CIA, but his sterling reputation as a first-rate professional accompanied him. Rumors circulated that Philby could well become the next chief of the SIS.

What transpired in Albania vividly demonstrated the lethal impact of Philby's conspiratorial work. In 1946, the SIS devised a plan to remove the new communist regime of Enver Hoxha from power and combined forces with the CIA three years later. With Marshal Tito distancing Yugoslavia from the USSR and Hoxha's dictatorship on shaky legs, the tide seemed to be running against Moscow in the Balkans. But as the joint coordinator, Philby had no difficulty in alerting the Soviets to the details of the operation, including the first land and sea infiltrations beginning in October 1949. At least 300 people died as a result. A further repercussion was the CIA's reluctance henceforth to assist in paramilitary operations in communist-ruled countries within the Soviet orbit. For different reasons, both sides found it in their interest to remain silent about the Albanian episode. It was also omitted from Philby's later memoir – *My Silent War* – even though it must be reckoned as one of his major coups.

The defection of Guy Burgess, who had been lodging with Philby and his wife in Washington, placed him under immediate suspicion. General Walter Bedell Smith, head of the CIA, tersely demanded his recall by London in June 1951: "Fire Philby or we break off the intelligence relationship."[5] Following his prompt retirement from the SIS, he survived two judicial inquiries by MI5 and – not lacking loyal supporters among his former colleagues – was assigned a minor post in the Middle East in 1956. Increasingly prone to drunken depressions and unwilling to accept a plea agreement, Philby decided to flee from Beirut to Moscow in early 1963 and remain there with his new Russian wife until his death 25 years later. Yet, to his chagrin, the KGB leadership never fully trusted him and refused to grant him officer rank, despite his reputation as its most illustrious and productive Western agent. In addition, the Philby affair injected much bitterness and suspicion into the Anglo-American intelligence relationship that was not soon overcome.

The announcement that the Soviet Union had successfully detonated its first atomic bomb on August 29, 1949 proved a deep shock to the Western public. The idea of producing a weapon of mass destruction involving uranium had originated as a joint wartime endeavor between US and British scientists under the auspices of the Manhattan Project. After witnessing the atomic bomb used against Japan by the Americans in August 1945 – and realizing its profound implications – Joseph Stalin decided to place the fledgling Soviet nuclear program (code name ENORMOUS) in the hands of his security and intelligence chief, Lavrenti Beria. According to his instructions, time was pressing, and no resources should be spared to insure its success. While prisoners from the Gulag supplied the necessary labor, Beria felt determined to construct a bomb utilizing the American model rather than settling for a cheaper Soviet version. The Manhattan Project thus became a prime target of Soviet espionage.

In spite of stringent security measures by US counterintelligence agencies, a number of key spies escaped initial scrutiny. One was Klaus Fuchs, a German-born physicist who had emigrated to Great Britain after 1933 and whose communist commitment had led him to volunteer his services to the Soviet Union. Another was Theodore Hall, a young American prodigy from New York fearful that his country was headed on a direct path to fascism. Two additional Americans included Julius Rosenberg, an ardent member of the CPUSA, and David Greenglass, a young military machinist on the Manhattan Project and likewise a devoted communist. That Fuchs and Hall were working independently of one another gave their Soviet controllers an added measure of confidence regarding the reliability of the secret scientific data that they had passed on. Their ultimate fates form a dramatic contrast. While under dogged interrogation by a British MI5 investigator, Fuchs confessed, explaining how his Marxist philosophy had been used to create two separate compartments in his mind, resulting in what he termed "controlled schizophrenia."

In the trial that followed, he was convicted of having violated the British Official Secrets Act and, after serving nine years of his 14-year sentence, left Britain for a scientific career in communist East Germany (he maintained that his loss of British citizenship was his deepest wound). Hall, quite remarkably, not only managed to escape prosecution by stonewalling the FBI but, with new research interests, found a position in Britain as a biophysicist at the Cavendish Laboratory at Cambridge University. When knowledge of his role as a Soviet spy became public in 1995, Hall merely reaffirmed his earlier views with no trace of regret.

The cause célèbre among the atomic bomb spies turned out to be the Rosenbergs, Julius along with his wife Ethel. After attending engineering school at City College of New York, he was enlisted by Soviet intelligence in 1942. Soon his duties involved managing an extensive espionage network with the assistance of his wife, although both of them refrained from further public agitation on behalf of the Communist Party. Ultimately, it was the confessions to the FBI by Greenglass, one of his principal recruits, that led to the joint trial of the couple in March 1951 (he was also married to the sister of Ethel).

Steadfastly denying and obfuscating as mandated by the party in such circumstances, the Rosenbergs successfully resisted the prosecutors' efforts to obtain more names. The couple contended that it was simply their "progressive" views that had compelled them to oppose the "fascist" warmongering of the Truman administration. A new strategy then sought to place Ethel on the same footing as her husband, despite the relatively minor role she had played, but Julius revealed no impulse to come to the aid of his wife by agreeing to cooperate with the prosecution. Pronounced equally guilty of a transgression "worse than murder" by presiding judge Samuel Kaufman – and having exhausted their legal appeals – they were both executed at Sing Sing Prison in New York on June 19, 1953. The couple had the distinction of being the only Soviet spies ever sentenced to death in the West.

News of the Rosenbergs' fate spread rapidly throughout the world and sparked an impassioned controversy that has lingered for decades. Their defenders felt emboldened by the eloquent manner in which they had protested their innocence to the very end and pointed to certain irregularities in the court proceedings. Yet, important evidence confirming their role as noteworthy Soviet spies has continued to accumulate. In addition to the Venona decryptions in which Julius appears under the code names ANTENNA and LIBERAL, a memoir of Nikita Khrushchev released in 1990 gratefully credited the couple with providing "very significant help in accelerating the production of our atomic bomb."[6] A subsequent firsthand account by Alexander Feklisov, the KGB case officer for both Fuchs and the Rosenbergs, was likewise full of praise, noting that "Julius saw his collaboration with Soviet intelligence as a kind of religious calling."[7] Then, in 2008, Morton Sobell, after having served a 16-year prison term in connection with the Rosenberg case, admitted that their primary motivation had been loyalty to the Soviet Union, not opposition to fascism as claimed by their defenders.[8]

From the Soviet point of view, Operation ENORMOUS has to count as one of the resounding successes of the early Cold War. Thousands of pages of vital high-level scientific and technical data had been obtained – not only via Fuchs, Hall, and Greenglass, but by other figures such as Russell McNutt, Boris Podolsky, Engellbert Broda, Melita Norwood (Britain's longest serving Soviet spy), and Allan Nunn May. This extensive information thus enabled the Soviet Union to bypass countless hours of laboratory experimentation and to minimize the vast financial investment normally required for such an endeavor. It hardly seems coincidental that the bomb that the Soviets exploded on August 29, 1949 was a plutonium model with an implosion detonator – a replica of the bomb that the United States had dropped on Nagasaki on August 9, 1945. Whereas Stalin and Beria proudly rewarded the Soviet scientists assigned to the project, the intelligence officers who had secured the closely guarded secrets from the West went generally unacknowledged.

Spy trials also made major headlines in the new "people's democracies" of Eastern Europe. Beginning in May 1949 with the arrest of László

Rajk, the Hungarian interior minister, ostensibly loyal communist officials throughout the Soviet satellite states came under suspicion for having engaged in treasonous behavior and were subjected to grueling repetitious interrogation designed to produce acute psychological disorientation. The list rapidly grew to include Gábor Peter, the founder and head of the Hungarian secret police; Wladyslaw Gomulka, the general secretary of the Polish Communist Party; Rudolf Slánský, the general secretary of the Czechoslovak Communist Party; Paul Merker, a prominent member of the East German politburo; Ana Pauker, the Romanian foreign minister; and Koçi Xoxe, the Albanian interior minister. Although some such as Gomulka and Merker were spared a public trial, the net cast often extended down the chain of command. Not only was Slánský found guilty and executed but ten other members of the Czechoslovakian party shared the same fate. Completely broken, Slánský quietly thanked his executioner for giving him "what I deserved."[9] The well-rehearsed one-week trial had been broadcast live by Radio Prague, and a printed transcript was widely distributed afterward.

Oddly, the connecting link among these officials was Noel Field, an American enlisted by Hede Massing as a Soviet spy during the mid-1930s while working for the US State Department. For the Soviets, his profile apparently contained what was needed to fabricate a vast full-blown conspiracy. During World War II, having earlier left government service, Field was based mostly in Geneva, helping refugees from the Third Reich – many of them fellow communists – under the auspices of the Unitarian Service Committee. He also had contact with Allen Dulles, the OSS chief in Switzerland at the time, in an effort to coordinate their anti-Nazi contacts. Then, in spring 1949, after being dismissed by the church organization because of his communist ties – and fearful of returning to the United States because of his intimate friendship with Alger Hiss, then enmeshed in his own legal troubles – Field found himself searching for new employment in Eastern Europe as either a freelance journalist or academic. Moscow became convinced that Field was working undercover for Western intelligence.

He and his wife, after being captured in Prague, were imprisoned in Budapest, his brother in Poland, and his foster daughter in the Soviet Union. Field's coerced admission of the charges against him, at the hands of the NKVD, unleashed a torrent of new accusations. Anyone in communist Europe who had ever encountered the man, however briefly, could be charged with abetting enemy intelligence. As the East German government commented, "The method used by Noel H. Field demonstrates the craftiness with which the enemy is able to smuggle its agents into the ranks of the Communists and labor unions."[10] And in their elaborate self-condemning confessions – scripted in Moscow and reminiscent of the Soviet show trials of the 1930s – Rajk, Slánský, and countless others specifically cited Field's influence as having been a precipitating factor in their own nefarious deeds. For the populace at large, the staging of these events served to reinforce the view promoted by the secret police throughout the Eastern bloc that all foreign contacts most likely involved espionage (the court proceedings against Rajk and his "fellow conspirators" including his confession were broadcast live on Radio Budapest). Never tried himself, Field was released from prison once the purges had ended following Stalin's death in 1953. Along with his wife, he was granted political asylum in Hungary. When questioned by Western reporters, he stated that the episode was merely a misunderstanding and he never abandoned his pro-Soviet allegiance, even when Red Army tanks rolled into Budapest a few years later.

Paris was the scene of yet another influential trial of the period.[11] It centered on Victor Kravchenko, a Soviet engineer and mid-level bureaucrat who had defected to the United States in 1944 while part of a visiting Lend Lease purchasing commission. Because of the publicity emanating from a well-attended press conference arranged by two American journalists on his behalf, the US government decided to ignore Soviet demands for his immediate return. Kravchenko next wrote a critical account of his life under Stalinism entitled *I Chose Freedom: The Personal and Political Life of a Soviet Official*, not knowing that one of his typists and one of the translators were both KGB agents. Published in 1946, the book became an immediate bestseller and was eventually translated into 22 languages – much to the distress of officials in Moscow.

When the French edition appeared the following spring – selling more than 250,000 copies – the pro-communist literary weekly *Les Lettres françaises* went on the offensive. In a lead article, Kravchenko was characterized as an alcoholic and a saboteur. Moreover, it accused the OSS of having arranged his defection and then hiring "Menschevik friends" to write his book since his own fumbling attempts had proven inadequate. Kravchenko responded by suing the magazine for defamation.

Gaining worldwide attention, the two-month trial took place in the Palais de Justice and was attended by hundreds of spectators, including major public and intellectual figures of the period. Kravchenko – determined not only to restore his reputation but to expose what he called "the horrors of Soviet reality" and force the Kremlin "to answer for all its crimes" – thus called as witnesses former Gulag inmates who had experienced firsthand the Stalinist atrocities of the previous decade. The case for the defense – which featured testimony by Maurice Thorez, the head of the then powerful French Communist Party – paled by comparison, especially when Kravchenko's hostile ex-wife turned out to be a perjurer and the alleged American author of the French article non-existent. In April 1949, the French court ruled in favor of Kravchenko and imposed nominal fines on *Les Lettres françaises* and its editors. It further stipulated the reimbursement of court costs and the publication of the verdict on the front page of the journal in standard-sized print. A second book by Kravchenko recounting the dramatic course of the libel trial appeared the following year.

Apart from the loss of its atomic bomb monopoly, another notable setback for the United States occurred with the multi-pronged invasion of South Korea by forces from North Korea on June 25, 1950. It was a stunning bolt from the blue for officials in the Truman administration. Although they had contemplated the high probability of an armed Soviet offensive somewhere in the world – and had methodically run a series of exercises on that assumption – the most likely flashpoints, according to Secretary of State Dean Acheson, appeared to be Turkey, Greece, Iran, and Berlin, especially after the recent blockade of the city (Soviet intelligence, for its part, had severely understated the Berlin airlift's chance of success and confidently but incorrectly predicted a speedy withdrawal of the Western powers). Korea, by contrast, had been discarded as a possibility, if only because of the nearness of US military bases in Japan and the seeming superiority of the South Korean army over its northern counterpart.

The lack of advance warning can be traced primarily to the failure of SIGINT, which bore a curious similarity to the defects in American operations that had preceded the Japanese attack on Pearl Harbor in December 1941. Following the end of the war, this crucial intelligence branch had been seriously underfunded and understaffed. Morale had declined significantly, compounded by keen rivalries among the three armed services and the lack of a coordinated command structure. A rapid expansion of SIGINT activities took place after the outbreak of hostilities on the Korean peninsula; but even then, another major surprise occurred five months later when officials received only fragmentary advance warning of the intervention of 300,000 Chinese troops that managed to repel the advancing UN forces. During the remainder of the stalemated conflict, duplication of effort and other wasteful practices continued to plague American SIGINT operations, even though several technological advances had been made, notably the introduction of aerial color photography to track enemy troop movements with greater precision. The ultimate reform came near the end of the Truman administration – November 4, 1952 – when the president, heeding the recommendations of a special investigative committee, signed an eight-page top-secret memorandum that brought the National Security Agency into existence.

The overriding challenge facing the Americans involved Soviet intelligence collection. In March 1953, DCI Allen Dulles freely admitted serious shortcomings during a meeting of the National Security Council. One stroke of good fortune, however, had recently occurred in Vienna where Pytor Semyonovich Popov, a young but rising GRU officer, volunteered his services to the Americans. Possessing mixed motives – resentment of the treatment accorded his peasant family in the USSR, the attraction of a Western lifestyle, and his fondness for his American handlers – he became the CIA's most important asset for the next five years. Besides supplying detailed information about Soviet espionage networks in the West, Popov produced documents on military policy toward NATO and Germany, thereby saving the United States at least US$500 million in its scientific and technical programs. Because of his importance, Dulles briefed Eisenhower personally about the case and brought along sample documents. Yet mounting suspicion by Soviet counterintelligence led to Popov's arrest and interrogation in February 1959. For eight months afterward, Popov continued to operate under Soviet control until he and his CIA handler were apprehended on a Moscow bus. Following a well-rehearsed secret trial, Popov was executed by a firing squad.

To help remedy the inadequacy of its human collection, the CIA directed its energies toward an array of technical measures. A most ingenious example took shape in Berlin in the form of a 500-meter underground tunnel extending from the American sector into the Soviet zone. Dubbed Operation GOLD and conducted jointly with the British SIS (who designated it STOPWATCH), it had been inspired by a similar endeavor in Vienna (Operation SILVER) when that city was likewise divided into occupation zones. The objective was to tap major phone lines leading to the Soviet military and intelligence headquarters at Karlshorst. A host of engineering obstacles presented themselves, not least the extremely sandy soil of Berlin, which necessitated lining the entire length of the excavation with heavy steel plates. To disguise the construction, a German contractor had built a large compound on the American side replete with a parabolic antenna to give the appearance of a radar station. The US Corps of Army Engineers completed the 6-foot-diameter tunnel in late February 1955, allowing the British to make the actual tap into the phone lines.

Even though early knowledge of the tunnel had been passed on to the Russians by British double agent George Blake, the intelligence yield during its 14 months of operation proved exceptional and shed light on a wide range of pressing topics. Weekly planeloads of tapes were flown out of West Berlin for careful analysis in Washington and

London. Considered most valuable were not specific secrets but acquiring a fuller understanding of the Soviet military's priorities, its communications network, and its plans for building East German and Polish military forces. Apparently fearful that Blake might be compromised should any countermeasures be undertaken, Soviet authorities had allowed the landline transmissions to continue until their stage-managed "discovery" of the tunnel in April 1956. While the Soviet ambassador in East Berlin promptly issued an official protest to the US commander, the American media trumpeted the achievement, calling it an example of "Yankee ingenuity" and "money well spent." Afterward, the site featured guided GDR propaganda tours and became East Berlin's most popular tourist destination. But neither side openly acknowledged the British contribution, especially that of SIS officer Peter Lunn, who could claim credit for the original concept developed in Vienna and supplying his indispensable expertise during the Berlin operation.

At the same time, another significant American advance was in the offing – this time high in the stratosphere rather than 16 feet below ground. Roughly seven months after the closing of the tunnel, Eisenhower approved a top-secret plan to build 30 state-of-the-art aircraft under the auspices of a CIA team headed by Richard Bissell. Equipped with new high-definition cameras, these one-man planes – popularly known as U-2s – were designed to fly at altitudes that would elude precise radar detection and be invulnerable to existing Soviet air-defense missiles and fighters (Soviet Air Force publications called the sleek aircraft "the black lady of espionage"). Following several trial runs, a U-2 made its initial voyage over the Soviet Union on July 4, 1956, and returned – unscathed but not undetected – to its air base in Wiesbaden, Germany. Despite the clear breach of international law and the periodical protests of Soviet officials through diplomatic channels, the surveillance flights took place on a frequent basis, producing a wealth of intelligence data concerning atomic plants, launching pads, and intercontinental missile activity. By 1959 – Bissell claimed – they were responsible for 90 percent of the agency's hard intelligence about the Soviet Union. Even an automobile license plate could not escape photographic detection.

But Eisenhower began to express growing concern over the risk of an incident and his own effectiveness at the negotiating table with the Soviet premier. Although the program had gone somewhat dormant, one more mission – deemed crucial and set for May 1, 1960 – received his authorization. Having rapidly developed an improved anti-aircraft missile in the meantime, the Soviets managed to bring the plane down near Sverdlovsk, their main atom research center, and capture its pilot, Francis Gary Powers. Confusion clouded both sides at first. Bissell assured the president that no pilot could survive (hence the erroneous US report of a "weather research" aircraft lost over Turkey), while Khrushchev produced photographs of the wrong wreckage during his initial speech before the Supreme Soviet.

Even though the Soviet leader took care not to blame Eisenhower directly, but rather "militarists in the Pentagon and the CIA," the president decided to hold a press conference and assume personal responsibility for the flights. In justifying his approval of the U-2 program, he stressed the "fetish of secrecy and concealment" that had developed in the USSR and the enormity of Soviet espionage operations in comparison to those of the Americans. Admittedly "distasteful," intelligence-gathering activities, Eisenhower asserted, were nevertheless "a vital necessity."[12] It was the first statement to the general public by an American president justifying the importance of peacetime intelligence-gathering operations. Aides had recommended the dismissal of top intelligence officials to show that Eisenhower was the victim of "over-zealous subordinates," but he resisted, believing that his main error lay in permitting the initial cover story.

When the two men next met at a five-nation summit in Paris in mid-May, Khrushchev angrily seized the initiative and demanded an apology, which Eisenhower calmly and unequivocally refused to make. To most observers, it was the Soviet leader's strident provocations – probably in deference to hardliners at home – that had caused the summit to collapse before it began. But his belligerence was to no avail, for he returned to Moscow with diminished status in the Kremlin hierarchy, while the American president received a hero's welcome from a throng of 250,000 persons lining Washington's Pennsylvania Avenue. As a result of the incident, the U-2 reconnaissance flights never resumed over the USSR, but they persisted for more than 30 years in many other parts of the world.

To continue the aerial surveillance of the Soviet Union, a revolutionary space-based collection system was devised by the CIA in conjunction with the US Air Force and private industry. Under the code name CORONA, the project produced the first photoreconnaissance satellite, capable of recording images on film and then ejecting a reentry capsule containing the film to earth for analysis. In August 1960 – after a number of failed mission attempts – *Discoverer XIV* succeeded in acquiring more overhead footage than the combined four years of U-2 coverage (the 84-pound capsule was recovered in midair over Alaska). Although the United States never relinquished its technological lead, the

Soviets were not far behind with their own program under the production code name ZENIT. In April 1962, *Cosmos 4* was launched possessing the ability to view locales of interest throughout the United States. Thus began a new technological era, which many claimed would reduce error and uncertainty in assessing military capabilities on both sides. Nonetheless, as was soon evident, major confrontations between the superpowers showed no signs of diminution for the foreseeable future.

Notes

1 John Earl Haynes and Harvey Klehr, *Early Cold War Spies: The Espionage Trials that Shaped American Politics* (Cambridge: Cambridge University Press, 2006), 234.
2 Robert J. Lamphere (with Tom Shachtman), *The FBI–KGB War: A Special Agent's Story* (New York, NY: Random House, 1986), 19–20.
3 Cited by Harry Howe Ransom, *The Intelligence Establishment* (Cambridge, MA: Harvard University Press, 1971), 163.
4 After the release of the American film *The Magnificent Seven* in 1960, the Center began to refer to them as the Magnificent Five.
5 Cited by John Ranelagh, *The Agency: The Rise and Decline of the CIA* (New York, NY: Simon and Schuster, 1987), 153.
6 *New York Times*, September 25, 1990.
7 Alexander Feklisov and Sergei Kostin, *The Man Behind the Rosenbergs* (New York, NY: Enigma Books, 2001), 120. See also http://www.pbs.org/redfiles/kgb/deep/interv/k_int_alexander_feklisov.htm.
8 *New York Times*, September 11, 2008.
9 Cited by Igor Lukes, "The Rudolf Slánský Affair: New Evidence," *Slavic Review*, 58(1) (Spring, 1999), 185.
10 Cited by Mária Schmidt, *Battle of Wits: Beliefs, Ideologies and Secret Agents in the 20th Century* (Budapest: XX Század Int., 2007), 165.
11 See Gary Kern, *The Kravchenko Case: One Man's War on Stalin* (New York, NY: Enigma Books, 2007).
12 Cited by E. Bruce Geelhoed, "Dwight D. Eisenhower, the Spy Plane, and the Summit: A Quarter-Century Retrospective," in Lori Lynn Bogle (Ed.), *Cold War Espionage and Spying* (New York, NY: Routledge, 2001), 257.

4 The Struggle Deepens

Nowhere was the dangerous collision course between the United States and the Soviet Union more evident to the world than in regard to the regime of Fidel Castro in Cuba. When John F. Kennedy was elected president in 1960, he wasted no time in making clear his determination to topple the recently installed "Maximum Leader." Preliminary plans, however, had already been formulated during the Eisenhower administration, inspired, to a considerable degree, by two successful CIA covert action operations in the recent past.

The first one in 1953 involved helping to unseat Muhammad Mussadeq, the Iranian prime minister who had nationalized British oil interests in the country after coming to power. By emphasizing instead the looming threat of Soviet expansionism into the region, the SIS secured the cooperation of the CIA, which then placed Operation AJAX in the hands of Kermit Roosevelt, a former OSS officer and the grandson of Theodore. The actual plan to topple Mussadeq originated in a group of Iranian politicians who considered his increasingly dictatorial stance in violation of the country's constitution. The pivotal event turned out to be the flight of the shah, as it spontaneously "galvanized the people," according to a CIA report, and led to Mussadeq's removal. The irate masses that occupied Tehran completely dwarfed the meager number of protesters financed by the CIA. From this episode, Roosevelt drew a crucial lesson: clandestine operations should only be attempted, as in this case, when most of the population and the army share the same goal as the agency. Otherwise, he stated, "give it to the Marines."

The second instance occurred shortly afterward in Guatemala, where the newly elected government of Jacobo Arbenz Guzmán had taken a number of provocative steps, including confiscating the holdings of the United Fruit Company and purchasing arms from the Soviet bloc. After an uncertain start – decisively aided by the use of black propaganda and air support – the forces of US-backed Colonel Carlos

Castillo Armas overthrew Arbenz, and the popular folk hero was installed as president in June 1954. US President Dwight Eisenhower unabashedly thanked Allen Dulles for averting "a Soviet beachhead in our hemisphere," and Armas made a two-week victory tour of the United States. Nevertheless, this blatant reassertion of the Monroe Doctrine left a bitter memory throughout Latin America, especially in light of the casualties and destruction caused by the bombing of civilian targets.

Drawing heavily from the underground experience of World War II, the Cuban plan first designed by the CIA task force headed by Richard Bissell envisioned a small number of refugees trained as guerillas who would be infiltrated into the country in order to join other guerilla or resistance groups. Kennedy appeared hesitant at first, but the persuasiveness of Allen Dulles, the current director of central intelligence, and Bissell, who was known for his exceptionally cogent presentations, won him over to the concept of an action-oriented policy. Under his direction, however, the covert action operation was dropped in favor of operation ZAPATA – a military invasion force of roughly 1,400 men, armed with tanks and supplied by ships, to be launched from the Bay of Pigs on April 15, 1961. Also receiving the president's approval, at least tacitly, was an assassination team that would target Castro in an "executive action" – an agency euphemism for the killing of foreign leaders.

Both ventures ended in utter failure. Within days of landing, many members of "La Brigada" had either surrendered or been killed, and two of the military transports were sunk by Cuban planes. In addition, the botulinum toxin pills given to a leading American mafioso to be relayed to a group stalking Castro never got near the intended victim. Why the invasion so quickly collapsed has sparked a variety of explanations. Some argue that such a foolhardy undertaking should have never been attempted in the first place, just as others contend that Bissell was too isolated and did not confer with colleagues in the analytical branch about the Cuban political situation. All the CIA personnel involved with ZAPATA agreed that air cover was an absolute prerequisite and that Kennedy's cancellation of the aircraft for the second strike – in the naive belief that public knowledge of American involvement would thereby be minimized – provided the fatal blow to the operation. When later asked by a newsman, Castro, too, replied, "They had no air support."[1]

While Kennedy made clear his accountability for the Bay of Pigs debacle, his obsession with Cuba appeared to grow even more pronounced. Prime responsibility for removing Castro from power now fell to his brother Robert, the attorney general, who began to prod the CIA into action again under the code name MONGOOSE. Applying unrelenting pressure and largely bypassing the new CIA chief, John McCone, who personally opposed assassinations, the younger Kennedy called it a "top priority ... all else is secondary." In 1962, a task force was formed in Miami employing 400 American staffers and 2,000 Cuban agents, thus becoming the largest CIA station worldwide. With another military action ruled out of the question, more than 30 different covert schemes were devised, all aimed at disrupting the government or damaging industry and agriculture but often bordering on the ludicrous with no possibility of realization.

The CIA further showed little appreciation for the rapidly growing prowess of the new Cuban agency – the Dirección General de Inteligencia (General Directorate of Intelligence, or DGI).[2] Well trained in the full range of illicit tradecraft by seasoned KGB instructors, the bulk of the initial recruits were eager young peasant and working-class revolutionaries possessing no nostalgia for the former Batista regime. They soon developed a particular expertise in creating double agents, turning CIA collaborators in other countries and manipulating them to their advantage. They also penetrated the Cuban émigré community in Miami and elsewhere with remarkable ease. Noteworthy is the fact that few agents received monetary payments, as most were motivated by their staunch ideological support for Castro's regime. Besides displaying their own firm devotion to their leader, members of the DGI felt immensely buoyed by the Bay of Pigs fiasco and already considered themselves superior to their American counterparts.

In Moscow, Nikita Khrushchev, who possessed a keen instinct for spotting weaknesses in others, concluded that Kennedy lacked the firm resolve that his office demanded – an impression confirmed at their first summit meeting in Vienna in June 1961. Thus emboldened, the Soviet leader continued to strengthen the USSR's military ties with Cuba, culminating in the installation of more than 40 medium- and intermediate-range ballistic rockets with nuclear warheads. It is noteworthy that Khrushchev made this decision without consulting the KGB, then under the lackluster chairmanship of Vladimir Semichastny, about the possible American response.

Fearing negative world opinion and a possible Soviet move against Berlin, the Kennedy administration – supported by the State Department – had stubbornly resisted the entreaties of the CIA to continue the regular U-2 overflights over Cuba during the critical five-week period of secret deployment. DCI John McCone ominously warned that this decision had created a serious void in intelligence collection – or what became known as the "photo gap" by administration critics.[3] Finally, on October 14, 1962, a single U-2 flight over western Cuba was authorized and confirmed the Soviet missiles in place and ready for firing. Via presidential envoys, the aerial photographs were shown to the leaders of France, West Germany, Great Britain, and Canada, and proved instrumental in securing their full support. Additional vital intelligence regarding the technical aspects of the Soviet missile program was supplied by an unusually important joint American and British agent, Colonel Oleg Penkovsky, deputy head of the foreign section of the GRU.

On October 22 – as tension mounted during the most perilous confrontation of the Cold War – Kennedy addressed the American public from the Oval Office, charging the Soviet government with "deliberate deception," announcing a quarantine on all offensive military equipment being shipped to Cuba, and demanding the removal of the existing missiles. While the speech contained no mention of the U-2 flights or any other form of intelligence-gathering, the US displayed its photographic evidence – to great effect – during a heated televised debate with the Soviet delegate in the United Nations Security Council. Fearing that his interests were being ignored, Castro defiantly pressed Khrushchev to counter with a massive preemptive nuclear strike against the United States if Cuba were invaded, but the Soviet leader rejected this unsolicited advice out of hand.

The resolution of the crisis came six days later, when Khrushchev agreed to dismantle all of the missile sites in Cuba in exchange for an American pledge not to invade the island. Fifteen US Jupiter missiles in Turkey were also removed as part of a secret understanding not revealed until many years later. Aerial inspections and covert action in Cuba resumed nonetheless, as the president called for a long-term plan to "keep pressure on Castro and bolster other regimes in the Caribbean." By fall 1963, the CIA had in place an even more aggressive "six-point integrated program against Cuba" calculated to incite the populace as much as possible and stimulate low-risk sabotage and resistance. Despite its peaceful outcome, the missile crisis had only propelled the level of enmity between Kennedy and Castro to new heights.

Berlin remained another global flashpoint. More than 80 different intelligence organizations operated there more or less independently, although the principal adversaries were four in number – the CIA at its base in the suburb of Dahlem, the KGB in Karlshorst, and the two opposing German services. Khrushchev, at various times, referred to Berlin as "a thorn," "a cancer," "a bone in my throat," even "the testicles of the West."[4] With East German citizens streaming to the West in ever increasing numbers – nearly three million had left since the GDR's founding in 1949 (one sixth of the total population) – Walter Ulbricht knew that his country's very survival was at stake. He therefore sought

Moscow's approval to erect a protective barrier at the borders of West Berlin and the FRG – one intended to stem not only the human exodus but also the flow of Western goods into East Berlin. Khrushchev, initially concerned about the reaction of the Western allies, finally gave his assent to a "steel ring" around the city once he felt assured that no countermeasures would result. Only a select handful of GDR officials including MfS chief Erich Mielke knew the full details of what was termed Operation ROSE. Deliberately excluded was the head of foreign intelligence, Markus Wolf, who, according to his autobiography, felt "pure professional fury," since no consideration had been given to the difficulties that his numerous agents and couriers would encounter at the newly sealed border nor to the advantages that would accrue to the enemy services.[5]

When Western leaders learned of the multilayered barbed-wire fence erected on August 13, 1961, nothing more than a verbal rebuke was uttered – much to the distress of West Berliners, including its outspoken mayor Willy Brandt who, in a letter to Jawaharlal Nehru, stated that "the barred walls of a concentration camp have now been erected inside Berlin."[6] Kennedy, on vacation in Hyannis Port, told his aides: "It's not a very nice solution, but a wall is a hell of a lot better than a war."[7] Prime Minister Harold Macmillan was likewise fearful of taking any action that could be interpreted as provocative by Moscow. Afterward, East German Security Secretary Erich Honecker, who had supervised the details of the operations, termed it "a defeat for Western intelligence," since most analysts believed that no move of this sort would occur before the signing of a separate peace treaty between the GDR and the Soviet Union scheduled for later that fall. Only with the reassurance that the West would remain passive did the construction of the densely fortified barrier – the so-called Wall of the First Generation – begin ten days later.

The following year the divided city attracted international attention once again but for a quite different reason. The first East–West spy exchange took place on the Glienicker Bridge, which connected West Berlin with Potsdam over the Havel River. Facilitated in large part by Wolfgang Vogel, East Germany's most prominent lawyer, Francis Gary Powers, the U-2 pilot downed over the Soviet Union in 1960, was exchanged for Rudolf Abel, a KGB colonel convicted in New York City in 1957 for having collected and transmitted national security information to the USSR and for residing in the United States as an illegal. More than two decades passed before a second exchange took place in June 1985. According to this arrangement, 25 spies held in Poland and East Germany were exchanged for four persons earlier apprehended by US authorities. In the final and most publicized instance less than a year later, Antoly Shchransky, a Soviet prisoner of conscience whom the Americans insisted was not a spy, was traded along with three other persons for five Eastern bloc operatives. Spy exchanges also became an ongoing part of the relationship between East and West Germany, but they usually took place at the Herleshausen-Wartha border crossing near Eisenach.

In 1968, shortly after the installation of Yuri Andropov as the new KGB chairman, the Soviet Union confronted a major challenge within the Warsaw Pact. During the so-called Prague Spring, reformist elements in Czechoslovakia under the leadership of Alexander Dubček had gained increasing prominence and relaxed many of the tight restrictions on free expression. Under the slogan of "socialism with a human face," economic reforms were instituted, and forums for political discussion expanded. For Andropov, the situation had a special poignancy, since as the earlier Soviet envoy to Budapest, he had played a pivotal role in the brutal suppression of the 1956 Hungarian revolution. This time, however, he urged "greater flexibility" in order to keep armed conflict to a minimum. Under Khrushchev, KGB espionage within the Eastern bloc had been forbidden, but that prohibition was now suspended, thereby allowing at least 30 illegals posing as visiting Westerners to operate freely in Czechoslovakia. Listening devices were also placed in the homes of reformist leaders.

Projecting a sophisticated manner rare for a Soviet official, Andropov nevertheless shared with his colleagues the deep-set conspiratorial belief that Western intelligence agencies ultimately stood behind these unsettling events, even in the face of contradictory evidence. The situation appeared all the more threatening because of the perceived unreliability of the Czech service, the StB, under Interior Minister Josef Pavel, who had himself taken a number of heretical steps. As the inner circle of the Soviet Politburo deliberated about how to proceed, it received a series of alarmist reports from Andropov designed to bolster the case for military intervention. Not only were traces of imperialist plots fabricated, but the KGB deliberately inflated the level of working-class support for Dubček's removal.

That members of the Warsaw Pact then decided to invade a "fraternal" country can, to a significant degree, be attributed to Andropov's influence. Even though the main military objectives were achieved within 24 hours – in contrast to the previous bloodshed in Hungary – the armed intervention inflicted permanent damage to the image of the Soviet Union well beyond the borders of Czechoslovakia. For Andropov, who was to become the longest serving KGB chief and the first to assume the leadership of the USSR, the lesson was clear. The Prague Spring had provided ample justification for the new Fifth Directorate created at his direction. Replete with 15 specialized departments, it was charged with developing the most effective means of combating what he called "ideological subversion inspired by our enemies abroad."[8]

Andropov also looked eagerly beyond the Eastern bloc to Latin America. Friendly relations were established in 1969 with the leftist government of Peru that extended to intelligence-sharing and the large-scale purchase of Soviet arms, but a similar attempt in Bolivia came to naught. As one of the most prosperous and stable countries in South America – and a lynchpin in Kennedy's Alliance for Progress program – Chile formed the biggest prize of all. The leader of the Chilean socialist party, Salvador Allende Gossens (code name LEADER), had attracted the attention of the KGB early in his career, and by 1961, he had consented to regular meetings as a "confidential contact" – a status below that of an agent. Despite his previous losses as a presidential candidate, Allende stood an improved chance of prevailing in the 1970 election since the anti-Marxist vote was split between two candidates.

Upon taking office, President Richard Nixon inherited a policy of both overt and covert opposition to the possibility of an Allende presidency. What was termed "non-attributable" assistance to designated Chilean political parties had actually begun as early as 1962, continuing on a stopgap basis but never forming part of a coherent strategy. In this instance – after much debate with the State Department – the CIA belatedly received authorization to engage in a "spoiling campaign" against Allende to break up his leftist Popular Unity coalition but not to lend direct support to either of the two other parties. These efforts costing US$425,000 had minimal impact and were easily eclipsed by more astutely targeted Soviet and Cuban actions. When Allende managed to win a razor-thin victory, Nixon – enraged by the outcome – was determined to keep him from being inaugurated at nearly any cost. Seeing no other alternative, the CIA reluctantly explored the possibility of assisting a military coup and established loose relations with a retired Chilean army general, Robert Viaux. An attempt to kidnap the Chilean chief of staff, General René Schneider, accidentally resulted in his death and the collapse of Viaux's ill-conceived plan before it had hardly begun.

During the next three years of Allende's presidency, US policy took a softer "cool but correct" stance. At a cost of roughly US$8 million, the new covert action program concentrated on supporting anti-government forces ranging from opposition political parties to the newspaper *El Mercurio* and trying again to sow dissension within Allende's already fractious coalition. The other main aspect involved monitoring indigenous coup plots without becoming active participants. While later critics severely doubted that such a distinction translated into actual practice, no evidence exists that the CIA or any other agency of the US government engaged in designing an overthrow of the regime with the Chilean armed forces. Through his flagrant mismanagement of the Chilean economy – the country's inflation in 1973 topped the world record at 190 percent – Allende not only faced mounting domestic opposition but had negated any large-scale support that might have come from Moscow. And despite his close relations with committed Cuban operatives, he failed to bring the armed forces and the security services under his direct control. In Andropov's view, Allende's main misstep was his reluctance to apply force against his opposition.

Given timely warning by the KGB, the Chilean leader escaped the first poorly organized coup attempt in June 1973. Conditions continued to deteriorate dramatically and led to the overthrow of his government three months later by his own appointment, General Augusto Pinochet, representing the three branches of the armed forces. From all indications, Allende – who had done little to prepare for this eventuality – took his own life, probably to minimize the bloodshed that he felt would inevitably follow. He quickly became a left-wing martyr throughout the world – aided by the KGB's active measures department. Many further believed that the coup had been engineered by the CIA and, in effect, turned a democracy into a brutal military dictatorship. A closer look at the record, however, shows that US intelligence had obtained no warning of the impending event until the day it occurred.[9] Pinochet, in fact, was a little known figure to the CIA – "a narrow-gauge military man," not a strong leader in its estimation.

Nixon, deeply suspicious of the CIA ever since his unsuccessful presidential campaign against Kennedy, soon found added justification for his low esteem. On October 6, 1974 – the Jewish holy day of Yom Kippur – Egyptian and Syrian forces advanced from separate directions to the utter surprise of the Israelis. Neither the American nor the Israeli intelligence services had thought such a military offensive at all likely for a host of reasons. Foremost was the swift defeat that Arab forces had suffered during the Six-Day War of 1967, which cast doubt on the fighting qualities of the soldiers themselves and strengthened the aura of Israeli invincibility. Any future Arab coalition, it was further assumed, would be unruly within its ranks. In addition, American military assistance to Israel since that time had increased substantially on the assumption that it would hasten a peaceful Middle East settlement.

President Anwar Sadat of Egypt, however, insisted upon the withdrawal of Israeli forces from the territory acquired during the 1967 conflict as a precondition to negotiations. Rebuffed by an Israeli refusal, Sadat believed that his only alternative was to return to the battlefield. Even when he spoke openly of his intention, intelligence professionals – with few exceptions – simply regarded these utterances as yet another example of Arab hyperbole. There was also no shortage of accurate signals intelligence owing to clandestine listening posts in the US embassies in Cairo and Damascus, but CIA analysts responsible for the Middle East were prone to dismiss these National Security Agency (NSA) intercepts out of hand. By contrast – most likely through its penetration of the Egyptian security services – the KGB managed to give advance warning to the Politburo of the Yom Kippur War. Its collection efforts in Israel, though, had suffered considerably since the severing of diplomatic ties in 1967.

After 20 days, Israeli counterattacks managed to halt the Egyptian and Syrian advance. Still, the toll exacted – 2,700 dead Israeli soldiers – was exceptionally high considering the country's total population, while the territorial losses included a section of the Golan Heights and part of the Sinai Peninsula. Prime Minister Golda Meir reluctantly appointed a government commission headed by the chief justice of the Israeli Supreme Court, Shimon Agranat, to investigate the intelligence failure – the *Mechdal* or "neglect" as it was commonly known. Despite being cleared of "direct responsibility," both Meir and Defense Minister Moshe Dayan resigned their offices under public pressure. There was also severe damage to the reputation of the country's celebrated intelligence community. But with the advent of the new government of Yitzhak Rabin came a new Mossad director, Yitzhak Hofi, who, when confronted with a hijacked Air France airbus containing many Jews and Israelis in June 1976, succeeded in laying the groundwork for a successful rescue operation at the air terminal in Entebbe, Uganda.

In Southeast Asia, the Nixon administration was also preoccupied by a longstanding conflict. Although the tangled roots of the Vietnam War predate the onset of the Cold War, direct US involvement in the region only began afterwards during the Eisenhower presidency. Following Ho Chi Minh's victory over the French in 1954, the Geneva Accords established a division of the country at the 17th parallel – a communist state under the Viet Minh took hold in the north, a US-sponsored anti-communist regime in the south. Still Eisenhower, firmly opposed to the deployment of American troops in what he considered a militarily disadvantageous peripheral area, endorsed only selective aid and other resources. The most notable American operative to arrive in Saigon was Edward Lansdale, who had just achieved a striking success in the Philippines combating the pro-communist Huk insurgency and stabilizing the US-supported government of Ramon Magsaysay. Dispatched by Allen Dulles of the CIA, he and his team of 12 were to wage "political-psychological warfare" against the enemy in conjunction with the South Vietnamese. But despite his special facility for working alongside Asians and listening sympathetically to their ideas, Lansdale's impact in Vietnam turned out to be noticeably more circumscribed.

Facing the formidable task of governing a highly fragmented South Vietnam was Ngo Dinh Diem, the anti-French son of a renowned mandarin who, as president, sought to preserve the core of Vietnam's traditional culture while modernizing the country with Western technology and science. Few gave Diem much chance of success. Yet after two years, US intelligence credited him with accomplishing "miracles."[10] Nearly one million impoverished refugees from the North had been absorbed; a constitution had been drafted along with a variety of social reforms; and he had largely neutralized opposition in the country, including plots by his own army. By 1955, South Vietnam was recognized *de jure* by 36 other nations. The authoritarian methods employed by Diem only reinforced his belief in the traditional Vietnamese view that a ruler must wield strength in order to be effective.

The CIA continued its careful tracking of developments in Vietnam. In addition – by the end of 1962 – it had created paramilitary units composed of 38,000 Uplanders, or Montagnards, who had fled their homeland to more secure government-controlled areas. The new president, John F. Kennedy, convinced that the loss of the country to the communists would have a fatal "domino" effect in the region, increased the number of US military advisors in the country and intensified covert action against North Vietnam, but ruled out the introduction of ground forces. Heeding the advice of Lansdale, he also remained generally supportive of Diem. Assurance was voiced in even stronger terms by Vice President Lyndon Johnson, who, after a tour of the region, proclaimed Diem to be the "Winston Churchill of Asia."

Yet, harsh criticism of Diem's autocratic methods steadily mounted among influential American journalists. He also raised the ire of the newly appointed US ambassador Henry Cabot Lodge, Jr., who urged a group of disgruntled generals to take matters in their own hands in light of Diem's seeming intransigence. John McCone, the director of central intelligence, counseled Kennedy against Diem's removal and warned of a "succession of coups and political disorder" in his absence.[11] McCone further stated his adamant opposition to any CIA involvement in an assassination plot. But Kennedy's first public criticism of the Saigon government – combined with his failure to take action against Lodge's violation of his own orders – led the generals to proceed with their coup. With the resulting deaths of Diem and his brother Nhu, McCone's bleak prediction soon came to pass. Moreover, the military progress in the war that had occurred under Diem, as even the North Vietnamese acknowledged, came to a halt, thus leading to the decision to deploy US ground forces in 1965.

Intelligence efforts directed at the North Vietnamese and the Viet Cong met with few successes. Kennedy, dissatisfied with the CIA's covert operation program, authorized the Defense Department to mount its own paramilitary campaign under the auspices of the Military Assistance Command Vietnam Studies and Observation Unit (MACVSOG) – the largest and most complex US undertaking since the days of the OSS during World War II. Apart from the inevitable rivalry that developed between MACVSOG and the CIA, all of the roughly 500 agents that both organizations inserted into North Vietnam to establish spy networks were quickly apprehended (some were even sent back as double agents). The record of the NSA turned out to be equally barren. Because the North Vietnamese and the Viet Cong had converted all of their communications to unbreakable cipher systems as early as 1962, US cryptanalysts were unable to read any of the enemy's high-level traffic. In addition, these systems were constantly changed and upgraded. It meant that operational intelligence might discern the broad contours of the conflict but not the enemy's actual strategy, combat methods, and organization.

Importantly, too, secret communist operatives working on behalf of the North Vietnamese and Viet Cong succeeded in gaining key positions in Saigon. One was Pham Ngo Thao, a colonel in the South Vietnamese army who was appointed by the Diem government to train the civil militia and to implement the country's new strategic hamlet program, which, in reality, he sought to subvert as much as possible. Another was Pham Xuan An, an affable journalist who had been purposely recruited to exert influence on the foreign press corps in Saigon. First as a stringer for Reuters and then as a correspondent for *Time* magazine, he achieved a reputation among American journalists as a prime source of inside information, especially regarding the South Vietnamese officer corps, and was, in turn, one of the few Vietnamese reporters admitted to off-the-record briefings by the US mission. Rumors even circulated that he was secretly in the employ of the CIA. Only after the conclusion of the war did the Americans learn of An's true communist allegiance.

Following Khrushchev's fall from power in 1964, the Soviet Union altered its posture and began to increase military aid to North Vietnam on a steady basis, becoming its largest supplier for the duration of the war. The KGB station in Hanoi also saw an immediate doubling of its personnel. Much of their effort focused on collecting and assessing air defense information in order to reduce the effectiveness of the US Rolling Thunder bombing campaign, principally through improved surface-to-air missile technology. Yet, because of the acrimonious Sino-Soviet split that had developed earlier in the decade, the Soviets were just as anxious to thwart the growing presence of the Chinese in the region. North Vietnam consequently became a central arena for Soviet espionage directed at the People's Republic of China.

For their part, the North Vietnamese showed little desire to subordinate themselves to either Moscow or Beijing. KGB officers assigned to Hanoi, to their frustration, had few opportunities to interrogate American prisoners of war or to gain access to captured enemy technology. Despite verbal assurances of fraternal solidarity between the two countries, the North Vietnamese interior minister and head of intelligence repeatedly rebuffed KGB chairman Vladimir Semichastny when approached regarding these matters. In this difficult working environment, there were further complaints about close surveillance by North Vietnamese counterintelligence as well as the many obstacles in recruiting agents from the local population.

The United States confronted a strategy against which its civilian and military leadership seemed conspicuously ill prepared. The communist enemy was willing to absorb large losses of manpower if an important psychological advantage could be gained. It also effectively relied on the traditional Vietnamese practice of *danh va dam* ("fighting and talking") in order to stimulate the opponent's "internal contradictions" and nullify its propaganda efforts.[12] According to the multipronged strategy of North Vietnam's commanding general, Vo Nguyen Giap, a protracted war would only intensify protests by the American public and the international community against Washington's official policy.

Many consider the turning point of the war to be the so-called Tet Offensive. On January 31, 1968 – during the Tet (or New Year) holiday – some 80,000 North Vietnamese and guerilla forces began a massive attack on more than 100 cities, military installations, and government facilities throughout South Vietnam. That the scale and intensity of this assault was not anticipated by the Americans must rank as the greatest intelligence failure of the war – comparable to the surprise attack on Pearl Harbor in 1941. A shrewd diversionary deception by Giap had led US intelligence to believe that the main military offensive would occur along the northwestern border of the country, notably at Khe Sanh. To analysts and senior commanders alike, it appeared almost certain that the enemy was attempting to duplicate its previous victory over the French at Dien Bien Phu in 1954. In relying on this analogy, these analysts (with one notable exception at the CIA) largely disregarded captured documents and prisoner interrogation reports, preferring to place their trust in SIGINT evidence, which failed to detect the Viet Cong forces units that had quietly begun to infiltrate the southern cities.

When the offensive ended in late February, the North Vietnamese had suffered disproportionate losses – roughly 58,000 men, including a generation of the best-trained Viet Cong fighters – and had failed to retain control over the urban areas with the exception of Hue. The spontaneous uprising among the South Vietnamese that Giap had anticipated never materialized as well. Yet, in psychological terms, a major victory had been scored by shattering American resolve at home. In its aftermath, President Johnson not only halted the bombing campaign in order to entice the North Vietnamese to the negotiating table; he also decided not to run for reelection that fall. In addition, the more optimistic estimates of enemy forces prepared by the Military Assistance Command Vietnam in the Department of Defense came under heavy criticism. By not taking full account of guerilla-militia elements in their computer models, these analysts had wrongly implied that the enemy lacked the capacity to mount a major offensive. CIA officials felt no small measure of vindication in that their more inclusive calculations had hewed closer to reality.

Following Tet, an intensified effort was made to destroy the formidable political infrastructure of the Viet Cong, primarily through the so-called Phoenix Program (*Phung Hoang* in Vietnamese). Devised by Robert Komer, a former analyst, and loosely connected to the CIA but carried out by the South Vietnamese, it sought to identify and remove Viet Cong personnel hidden in the civilian population at every level from the most isolated hamlet to the urban enclaves of Hanoi. Owing to some of the harsh interrogation methods employed and the number of deaths that resulted, it aroused intense criticism by anti-war protesters in the United States. Its defenders, however, reject the charge that Phoenix constituted an assassination program targeting civilians. They note that the American advisors never sanctioned extreme torture or executions – the CIA's preferred method of interrogation, according to one officer, was "painstaking, patient questioning, checking and requestioning in circumstances calculated to emphasize the prisoner's helplessness and dependence on his captors"[13] – and that the vast majority of the fatalities involving the Viet Cong infrastructure occurred during skirmishes and raids by the South Vietnamese and US military, often because of the intelligence that had been extracted. Moreover, by the time the program ended in 1971, the elimination of some 65,000 activists – more than a quarter having opted for amnesty – meant that the Viet Cong had ceased to be a significant terrorist threat to the general population.

The next major chapter in the Vietnamese conflict occurred under the Nixon administration, when the focus shifted to neighboring Cambodia. The president's objective was to achieve an honorable negotiated settlement, which, he felt, necessitated demonstrating an unflinching commitment to the military struggle despite growing domestic opposition. Based on imagery obtained showing a large network of North Vietnamese base camps and supply depots, Nixon first authorized a secret bombing campaign (codenamed MENU) and later limited troop action. Yet, behind the scenes another intense debate took place between the Pentagon and the CIA – this time regarding the amount of Chinese-supplied *matériel* being transported through Cambodia. Although both groups were working from the same low-grade set of data, they arrived at quite different estimates. By late May 1970, as the North Vietnamese expanded their control over eastern Cambodia, the US and South Vietnamese forces withdrew from the country. The following year, an invasion was attempted in Laos, but, contrary to the CIA analysis indicating a weak North Vietnamese presence, the South Vietnamese army suffered a resounding defeat. The country's final struggle for survival began in January 1975 with an assault by North Vietnamese forces in the Phuoc Long province – an action completely misjudged by the CIA. But by late April, an all too accurate intelligence assessment delivered to President Gerald Ford, Nixon's successor, stated unequivocally that Saigon faced "imminent military collapse." Air America – the CIA's large secret fleet employed on a variety of wartime missions – assisted with the evacuation of the city and was dissolved the following year.

At home, the CIA came under increasing public scrutiny. It was specifically implicated in the Watergate affair that led to Nixon's resignation in August 1974; former CIA employees had formed part of the Plumbers unit, while the president had sought agency cooperation in the subsequent cover-up. Ford then had to confront what became the most intense public debate ever over the role of the American intelligence community – the so-called "time of troubles," as one ranking CIA officer called it. William Colby, the DCI at the time, bitterly complained in retrospect that "the CIA came under the closest and harshest public scrutiny that any such service has ever experienced not only in this country but anywhere in the world."[14] In December, the first major salvo came from the investigative journalist Seymour Hersh in the *New York Times*, charging the agency with violating its charter by conducting domestic surveillance of the antiwar movement during the Nixon and Johnson administrations. Attempting to placate public opinion, Colby responded by firing James Jesus Angleton, the legendary but controversial head of counterintelligence, and taking a relatively open, conciliatory stance toward Congress – a striking departure from his predecessors, especially Richard Helms, who preferred the traditional "silent service," volunteering nothing and answering questions tersely without elaboration. The consensus at headquarters also called for massive resistance. But the demand to have the agency divulge more of its innermost secrets – what it termed "the skeletons" and the press "the family jewels" – merely grew louder. By holding tenaciously to his belief that full exposure would work to the CIA's benefit in the long run, Colby acquired the reputation of being the most polarizing director in the agency's history (some irate former colleagues hinted to journalists that he might be a Soviet mole).

Three investigative commissions soon formed: a blue-ribbon presidential one under Vice President Nelson Rockefeller, the other two based in the Senate and House of Representatives. Gone were the days when the CIA operated under minimal Congressional oversight. Moreover – much to the consternation of veteran intelligence officers – the dark image that took hold among Americans in general was that of a "rogue elephant" – in the memorable phrase of Frank Church, the chair of the Senate committee. The list of aired CIA transgressions expanded to include under-the-table subsidies to friendly partisan groups overseas, a mail-intercept program, experiments with mind-altering drugs on unsuspecting individuals, the development of poisons and biological weapons, and the attempted assassination of foreign leaders – Fidel Castro and Patrice Lamumba of the Congo, in particular.

President Ford, however, showed no hesitancy in criticizing the seeming irresponsibility of the congressional committees, stressing that "the crippling of our foreign intelligence services increases the danger of American involvement in direct armed conflict."[15] The murder, too, of Richard Welch, the undercover CIA station chief in Athens, by masked gunmen in late December 1975 made a deep impression and clearly put the two committees on the defensive. The CIA claimed that prime responsibility lay with Philip Agee, an embittered former officer who, working with Cuban intelligence, had made public the names of hundreds of American covert operatives abroad (the CIA's first defector, despite remaining in the West, he later put the figure at roughly 2,000 officials exposed by him and his Soviet-backed team).

When the end finally came to this acrimonious tug-of-war involving assertions of executive privilege and contempt-of-Congress citations, nearly everyone could claim a partial victory. Of the various reforms put in place, the most far-reaching was the creation of permanent standing committees on intelligence oversight in both branches of Congress. According to the founding resolution, these committees should be kept "fully and currently informed with respect to intelligence activities." That meant, in practice, receiving finished intelligence, but not raw reporting or the highly classified *President's Daily Brief.* The Intelligence Oversight Act of 1980 further strengthened the original legislation, especially in the realm of covert action, thus making Congress an increasingly important player. No other major power in the world could match such a high degree of legislative authority and overall transparency in these matters.

At the same time, the six-volume final report of the Church committee published in April 1976 openly acknowledged the "important contributions" by members of the US intelligence community who had generally carried out their missions with "dedication and distinction." Even more satisfying for CIA officials was the conclusion of the House investigative committee: "All the evidence in hand suggests the CIA, far from being out of control, has been utterly responsive to the instructions of the President and the Assistant to the President for National Security Affairs."[16] Any past misdeeds, in other words, had emanated from the Oval Office, not CIA headquarters at Langley. Nevertheless, this episode marked the beginning of a persistent pattern that gave nearly any allegation of wrongdoing instant credibility in the public mind.

If the United States suffered a bitter defeat in Vietnam because of its poor understanding of indigenous forces, the Soviet Union fared no better in Afghanistan. Its direct involvement in the country began in April 1978, when a violent, well-rehearsed military coup led to the murder of the prime minister, Muhammed Daoud, and the installation of Nur Muhammad Taraki, the head of the pro-Soviet People's Democratic Party of Afghanistan (PDPA). Soviet influence could also be found in the country's army, as nearly one third of the officer corps had received training in the USSR, with many establishing a tie to the KGB and the GRU.

Even though Taraki had been recruited as a Soviet agent nearly 30 years earlier, once in power, he proved to be quite problematic from the KGB's perspective. Besides holding him responsible for a growing split within the PDPA between two rival factions – the Khalq (or "Masses") and the Parcham (or "Banner") – it found him to be overly pretentious in his self-styled role as the "Great Leader of the April Revolution," which combined the offices of president and prime minister. Yet, Taraki's main strategic error – one reinforced by the Soviet Union – was to attempt to impose communist rule on a largely tribal and staunchly

Muslim country with minimal popular support. In fact, he readily invoked the example of Lenin and his admonition to be merciless toward enemies of the revolution, real and potential. Not surprisingly, the Afghan security apparatus came under his direct supervision.

Initially underestimated by the KGB, resistance to the new regime quickly grew into a fully fledged *jihad* or holy war, against which Taraki's forces, plagued by desertions, seemed decidedly ill matched. His desperate request to Moscow for Soviet troops in disguise "to save the revolution" went unheeded, although it agreed to more military aid and advisors (a KGB detachment of roughly 150 men posing as embassy personnel was also dispatched to protect the compound in Kabul). While the insurgency continued to intensify, the situation was further compounded by a power struggle between Taraki and fellow Khalq, Hafizullah Amin, which resulted in the former's resignation in September 1978 and subsequent murder by suffocation. The KGB had even more serious reservations about Amin who, owing to his earlier studies in the United States, was rumored to be an American spy.

Fearing the expulsion of Soviet advisors by Amin and a sharp turn toward the West – what Andropov termed "ideological sabotage" – Moscow began to take more decisive action. By November, the KGB had selected another of its long-term Afghan agents, Babrak Karmal, to head a new proxy government. In strictest secrecy, preparations for a massive military invasion took shape accompanied by a KGB plan to assassinate Amin if necessary. Operation AGAT commenced late Christmas Eve and was concluded several days later. Although the KGB expressed general satisfaction with the outcome, more than 100 members of its special forces (*Spetznaz*) were killed or wounded before Amin and his entourage were fatally shot at the Darulaman Palace. In reporting to Soviet leader Leonid Brezhnev, the KGB falsely claimed that the assassination was primarily the work of the Afghans themselves and that it had the support of the working masses, the intelligentsia, and others in the army and state bureaucracy.

Andropov's goal of stabilizing communist rule in Afghanistan never occurred. Karmal began to develop the same self-inflated persona as Taraki, while the simmering factionalism in the party continued unabated. Realizing that a policing action was insufficient to neutralize the massive anti-Soviet reaction, Moscow ordered a more assertive role for its troops. Yet, because of its military commitments elsewhere, the Soviets could never deploy as many divisions as the Americans in Vietnam nor had the Red Army received training in the guerilla tactics as practiced by the *mujahadeen* (or resistance fighters). The Soviet thus conducted large-scale offensives against towns and villages believed to be affiliated with the guerillas, eventually forcing at least one third of the population to flee the country – what some observers called "migratory genocide." A new Afghan security force was also formed by the KGB and – under the command of Muhammad Najibullah, the country's future ruler – gained notoriety for treating its prisoners in a brutal manner reminiscent of the Stalin era.

As the military stalemate developed, Andropov held the United States and Pakistan as primarily responsible for the lack of Soviet success. Aided by accurate advance monitoring of the mobilization by American satellite imagery, President Jimmy Carter had responded immediately to the Soviet invasion and instructed the CIA to commence supplying arms via Pakistan to the *mujahadeen*. Covert support then took a quantum leap in the 1980s due largely to the efforts of Charles Wilson, a colorful Texas Democrat and a member of the House military appropriations subcommittee. Not content merely to see the Soviets pay a heavy price, Wilson was determined to see the Afghan guerillas prevail by using his behind-the-scenes Washington connections.

Under the direction of Gust Avrakotos – a maverick intelligence officer and ally of Wilson – the CIA provided increasingly lethal weapons that included tens of thousands of automatic weapons and antitank guns along with satellite intelligence maps – all transported across the Pakistani frontier on mules also procured by the Americans (direct contact between the CIA and the *mujahadeen* was deliberately avoided). Local expertise became the domain of the Pakistani Inter-Services Intelligence, and additional matching funds were secured from Saudi Arabia. Thanks to the vigorous advocacy of the CIA's Jack Devine, US aid culminated in the shoulder-fired, heat-seeking Stinger missile systems designed to counter the Soviets' highly destructive Hind Mi-24 helicopter gunships. Its longest and most expensive covert operation to date, Operation CYCLONE counted as one of the CIA's major successes, even though some critics noted that the whereabouts of numerous Stinger missiles was never ascertained after the Soviet withdrawal from Afghanistan in 1989.

Before leaving office, Carter had to confront the gravest crisis of his presidency. In early November 1979, several thousand young militant Iranian revolutionaries seized the embassy in Tehran, taking more than 50 US personnel hostage. It was an act that took Washington by surprise, just as earlier that year the overthrow of Shah Reza Pahlevi and the installation of the Islamic fundamentalist, Ayatollah Rouhallah Khomeini, had been completely unforeseen (a CIA assessment as late as August 1978 had detected no signs of revolutionary ferment). Khomeini, too, had not known in advance of the embassy takeover, but observing the eruption of popular sentiment against the "Great Satin," he eagerly utilized the event to consolidate the first radical Islamic regime in modern times.

The crisis for Carter gained added poignancy because of the unprecedented real-time imagery of the KH-11 satellite, which allowed him aerial views of the Tehran compound on a daily basis. After months of fruitless negotiations, the president finally agreed to a secret military rescue operation codenamed EAGLE CLAW. Within his administration, it was a controversial decision and prompted the resignation of his secretary of state, Cyrus Vance. Although officials carefully laid the groundwork by conducting a successful reconnaissance flight, the two-stage plan was an immensely complex one involving a combination of planes, helicopters, troops, and land vehicles. Most crucially, it permitted scant room for human or technical error. The fact that most of the CIA personnel stationed in Tehran counted among the hostages further diminished the chances of a positive outcome.

On the day of the operation – April 24, 1979 – Carter's initial optimism quickly turned to despair as he learned that two of the eight Marine Corps helicopters had failed to arrive at their designated desert station, another had developed a hydraulic problem, and, even worse, yet another had collided with an Air Force C-130 refueling aircraft, setting both on fire. It later came to light that eight servicemen and an Iranian interpreter were killed as a result. Reminded all too vividly of Kennedy's Bay of Pigs fiasco, Carter felt compelled to abort the mission. Subsequent assessments not only criticized the excessive reliance placed on high technology by the president and his team but pointed out that no full-scale rehearsal had taken place to ensure that all the various elements had been integrated into a coherent whole.

After 444 days in captivity, the American hostages were finally released; but to Carter's chagrin, the Iranians delayed the event until immediately after the new president, Ronald Reagan, had been inaugurated. Significantly, though, before his departure from the White House, Carter had revealed a major change of heart regarding the importance of covert action in the country's intelligence arsenal. In 1976, he had campaigned with undisguised hostility toward the CIA's activities in this realm, stating that "we always suffer" when they later come to light. A look at his record in office, however, reveals a surprising number of approved covert operations, not just against the Soviets in Afghanistan but also directed at Soviet-sponsored Marxist regimes in Angola, Ethiopia, Mozambique, and South Yemen. And at a press conference following his last State of the Union address, he candidly remarked, "There's been an excessive restraint on what the CIA and other intelligence groups could do."[17]

Before the decade was over, two of the Eastern bloc services suffered high-level defections that rank among the most consequential of the Cold War. The first occurred in July 1978 when Ion Mihai Pacepa, the deputy head of DIE, Romania's foreign intelligence division, requested political asylum in the United States while in West Germany negotiating a joint aircraft venture with Fokker. His departure precipitated a sweeping purge of Romanian officials. According to Pacepa, one third of the ruling Council of Ministers were demoted, 22 ambassadors replaced, and more than a dozen senior security officers arrested. DIE was subjected to a major reorganization, and its officers stationed abroad were recalled, some, however, preferring to defect instead.

A further blow to Romania's international reputation involved Pacepa's detailed revelation of Operation HORIZON. Personally conceived in 1972 by the country's obsessive dictator, Nicolae Ceauşescu, this influence operation sought to cultivate the image of a maverick anti-Soviet state in the communist bloc – "a Latin island in a Slavic sea," as he phrased it – in order to attract lucrative Western investments and advanced technology normally prohibited to communist countries. Traditional foreign intelligence activities were given secondary status so that DIE's dramatically increased personnel and budget could exploit every possible opportunity – from "documents 'signed' by heads of foreign governments, counterfeited in Bucharest and 'accidentally lost' in luxury hotels or leaked to the West in other ways" to "intelligence officers operating under the cover of the robes of ambassadors and archbishops."[18] That shrewd Western leaders such as Richard Nixon and Charles de Gaulle had had no qualms in embracing the Romanian ruler testifies to the effectiveness of HORIZON.

The other case concerned Werner Stiller, a rising officer in East German foreign intelligence who specialized in the recruitment of Western physicists. His growing disillusionment with the communist regime had led him to make contact with the West German BND. Fearing imminent exposure, Stiller devised an intricate and daring escape in January 1979 from the Friedrichstrasse Train Station to West Berlin, bringing with him approximately 20,000 microfilmed documents from Stasi headquarters. The resulting damage was immense. Besides giving Western officials their first detailed knowledge of the GDR's far-reaching scientific and technological espionage, his information resulted in the arrest of 17 agents in the Federal Republic (15 were warned in time and exfiltrated). In addition, Stiller was able to identify Markus Wolf, the head of East German foreign intelligence for the past two decades, from a photograph taken earlier in Stockholm. Until then he had been known among Western intelligence officials simply as "the man without a face."

Wolf characterized Stiller as "the only outright winner in one of the sorrier sagas of my career."[19]

Notes

1 For Castro's fuller appraisal, see Tad Szulc, *Castro: A Critical Portrait* (New York, NY: William Morrow, 1986), 557–558.
2 See Brian Latell, *Castro's Secrets: The CIA and Cuba's Intelligence Machine* (New York, NY: Palgrave Macmillan, 2012).
3 See David M. Barrett and Max Holland, *Blind Over Cuba: The Photo Gap and the Missile Crisis* (College Station, TX: Texas A&M University Press, 2012).
4 Cited by William Taubman, *Khrushchev: The Man and His Era* (New York, NY: W. W. Norton, 2004), 407.
5 Markus Wolf (with Anne McElvoy), *Man Without a Face: The Autobiography of Communism's Greatest Spymaster* (New York, NY: Times Books, 1997), 104.
6 Cited by Timothy Garton Ash, *In Europe's Name: Germany and the Divided Continent* (New York, NY: Random House, 1993), 59.
7 Cited by Kenneth P. O'Donnell and David F. Powers with Joe McCarthy, *"Johnny, We Hardly Knew Ye": Memoirs of John Fitzgerald Kennedy* (Boston, MA: Little, Brown, 1972), 303.
8 Cited by Andrei Soldatov and Irina Borogan, *The New Nobility: The Restoration of Russia's Security State and the Enduring Legacy of the KGB* (New York, NY: Public Affairs, 2011), 55.
9 See Kristian Gustafson, *Hostile Intent: US Covert Operations in Chile, 1964–1974* (Washington, DC: Potomac Books, 2007).
10 Martin Herz, *The Vietnam War in Retrospect* (Washington, DC: Georgetown University School of Foreign Service, 1984), 22–23.
11 Cited by Harold P. Ford, *CIA and the Vietnam Policymakers: Three Episodes 1962–1968* (Washington, DC: Center for the Study of Intelligence Central Intelligence Agency, 1998), 36.
12 See Truong Nhu Tang (with David Chanoff and Doan Van Toai), *A Vietcong Memoir: An Inside Account of the Vietnam War and Its Aftermath* (New York, NY, Harcourt Brace Jovanovich, 1985), 200–218.
13 Cited by Mark Moyar, *Phoenix and the Birds of Prey: The CIA's Secret Campaign to Destroy the Vietcong* (Annapolis, MD: Naval Institute Press, 1997), 105–106.
14 William Colby and Peter Forbath, *Honorable Men: My Life in the CIA* (New York, NY: Simon and Schuster, 1978), 391.
15 Cited by Christopher Andrew, *For the President's Eyes Only: Secret Intelligence and the American Presidency from Washington to Bush* (New York, NY: HarperCollins, 1995), 418.
16 Cited by Andrew, *For the President's Eyes Only*, 420.
17 Cited by Andrew, *For the President's Eyes Only*, 455. See also Robert M. Gates, *From the Shadows: The Ultimate Insider's Story of Five Presidents and How They Won the Cold War* (New York, NY: Simon and Schuster, 1996), 176–179.
18 Ion Mihai Pacepa, *Red Horizons: Chronicles of a Communist Spy Chief* (Washington, DC: Regnery Gateway, 1987), 9.
19 Wolf, *Man Without a Face*, 188.

5   Three Profiles of Cold War Spies

One might pause for a moment and ask the underlying question of what prompts a person into long-term, high-stakes espionage, particularly during the Cold War period. A well-known acronym MICE encapsulates the most basic motivations in the recruitment of spies: money, ideology, career, and ego. However helpful as a starting point, these four elements might well combine in an unanticipated manner and become compounded by additional factors such as a simple craving for adventure. Experience has further shown that there are myriad ways in which human spies adjust their behavior and seek to rationalize their actions. In any event, there can be little doubt that all of these individuals were no run-of-the-mill operatives and succeeded in making a deep imprint on their times for better or worse. The profiles that follow – an East German couple who penetrate the West German political establishment; an American who brazenly sells top secrets to the Soviet Union; and a Pole who becomes a leading informant for the United States – help bring into sharper focus the deeper and diverse psychological forces at play.

Günter and Christel Guillaume

Few figures better epitomize the highly conflicted relationship that developed between East and West Germany than Günter Guillaume and his wife Christel. Born in a workers' district of Berlin on February 1, 1927, he was the son of a silent film musician and a hairdresser. During the final year of the war, he served as youth conscript (*Flakhelfer*) and also joined the Nazi Party. Afterward, released from brief British captivity, Guillaume gained a position as a technical editor and photographer for Volk und Wissen, the East German state publishing house for educational and pedagogical materials as well as a front organization for the Ministry of State Security (MfS). In 1951, Christel Boom, the daughter of a Dutch merchant who had suffered persecution because of his defense of his

Jewish colleagues, became his wife. The following year he joined the Socialist Unity Party (SED).

Paul Laufer, a veteran communist, proved a persuasive mentor, and by 1955 Guillaume's connection with the MfS as a so-called "officer in special deployment" was sealed. He later remarked that his main motivation was to compensate for his wartime activities on behalf of the Nazis. To facilitate the "emigration" of the couple to the Federal Republic, Christel's mother, Erna Boom, who possessed a Dutch passport, left first and established herself in Frankfurt am Main with no difficulty. The Guillaumes followed in 1956, and by registering beforehand with Christel's mother, they avoided the espionage check that political refugees faced in the emergency shelters. Guillaume (code name HANSEN) took over his mother-in-law's small coffee and tobacco shop – Boom am Dom – while Christel (code name HEINZE) found employment as a secretary. Contrary to his later assertions, he had not received advanced systematic training in espionage prior to his arrival in the West.[1]

The Guillaumes' original assignment was a relatively modest one – to act as handlers for sources in the West German Social Democratic Party (SPD) on behalf of the Stasi's foreign intelligence division (HVA). On his own initiative, however, Guillaume pursued a much more ambitious course, not only joining the party but becoming a writer and photographer for the party's district chapter newspaper. Within a year, his full involvement allowed him to drop the cover of managing the small shop. Posing as an unabashed anti-communist – and not hesitating to advise against diplomatic recognition of the GDR – he found support among right-wing members anxious to assert themselves in the prevailing left-wing milieu. A series of local party positions followed, culminating in Guillaume's election to the Frankfurt city council in 1968. During this same period, as a secretary to a SPD Bundestag deputy and member of the party leadership, Wilhelm Birkelbach, Christel was acquiring even more valuable information, notably the description and evaluation of two different North Atlantic Treaty Organization (NATO) and Group North military exercises.

A major breakthrough in Guillaume's career occurred with the national elections in September 1969. Because of his skillful direction of the campaign of Georg Leber, a prominent conservative Social Democrat and labor union leader from Frankfurt, Guillaume was promised a position in Bonn. As Willy Brandt began to assemble West Germany's first socialist-led government, the name of Guillaume was enthusiastically advanced by Leber (who became labor minister and later defense minister). Although he vouched for Guillaume's "absolute trustworthiness," questions nevertheless arose regarding his security credentials. Several vague tips had, in fact, reached West Germany's investigative agencies, and an interrogation took place in early January 1970 led by Horst Ehmke, Brandt's chief-of-staff and an admitted novice in intelligence and security matters. While conceding his former membership in the GDR youth organization, the Freie Deutsche Jugend (Free German Youth), and the labor union, Guillaume pointedly denied any Stasi connection. All of the queries were answered in such a natural and confident manner that any lingering suspicion was easily put to rest. As he later stated, however, those two hours counted as among the most difficult in his entire career.

By the end of the month, the BfV (the Office for the Protection of the Constitution) had concluded that since nothing irregular could be found in his dossier, Guillaume could have access to documents up to the level of "secret." His new position as a junior aide in Brandt's office gave him responsibility for relations with the trade unions and other political organizations. Exceptionally eager and hardworking, yet also possessing a jovial down-to-earth demeanor, he continued his steady ascent. His immediate superior remarked that only rarely had he encountered anyone as outgoing and able to gain the confidence of those both above and below him. The only notable criticism Guillaume received came from some older civil servants who complained about his lack of a high-school diploma and experience in government service. In the meantime, his wife obtained a position with the Hessian state offices in the West German capital.

While in Frankfurt, Guillaume had maintained contact with East Berlin by passing information placed in empty cigar containers at his mother-in-law's store; his own instructions were relayed by coded shortwave radio messages. But in Bonn, he preferred to meet with two highly experienced couriers – codenamed ARNO and NORA – in nearby restaurants, hotels, and automobiles, rarely conveying written documents or photographs but delivering his insider knowledge orally. Such contacts were deliberately kept at a minimum. Most prized by the HVA was his assessment of the Brandt government's policy of *Ostpolitik* – the attempt to achieve a rapprochement with the Eastern bloc, especially the GDR and the Soviet Union. His chief value lay in hearing what was being said informally behind-the-scenes, catching moods and nuances that documents rarely reveal.

Guillaume reached the pinnacle of his career in the summer of 1972 when one of Brandt's three top personal aides decided to run for office himself. Appointed to this vacancy – and receiving an upgraded security clearance – the East German operative quickly became known among colleagues as "Brandt's shadow," especially during the successful fall reelection campaign as they crisscrossed the country in the chancellor's special train. No task was considered too trivial – whether fetching fresh croissants for breakfast or selecting properly matched attire for official occasions. When any disparaging remarks reached his ears, Guillaume came unhesitatingly to his boss's defense. The chancellor, however, harbored distinct reservations about his new personal assistant. Despite praising "his zeal for service (*Diensteifer*) and his skillfulness in organizational matters," Brandt nevertheless disliked his mixture of "servility and chumminess" and thought him too intellectually limited for serious political discussions. He had even voiced his desire to have him reassigned to a more distant area of responsibility.

Yet before that could occur, the chancellor was informed in spring 1973 of new leads that implicated his personal assistant. In the course of pursuing another case, a counterintelligence investigator began to assemble pieces of circumstantial evidence that pointed in the direction of Guillaume and his wife. Most persuasive were intercepted and decrypted radio transmissions dating from the 1950s. To bolster the morale of those stationed abroad, the HVA had followed the practice of sending coded greetings on birthdays, holidays, and family occasions. On this basis, the investigator ascertained a direct link with both Guillaumes along with the birth in 1957 of Pierre, their only child. This finding gradually reached the head of BfV, Günther Nollau, who in turn notified the interior minister, Hans-Dietrich Genscher. When informed himself, Brandt reacted with incredulity – "completely far-fetched" given Guillaume's previous security clearances – although he took no issue with Nollau's recommendation that his personal assistant remain in place and be kept under confidential surveillance. The evidence collected thus far would hardly suffice in a court of law.

The following weeks yielded no additional proof of Guillaume's double role, possibly because the surveillance was purposely limited to his off-duty hours. Brandt presumably tested his aide as well by occasionally leaving carefully ordered papers and pencils on his desk in the evening to see if they had been altered the next day. In early July, when the chancellor began his vacation at Harmar in the Norwegian countryside north of Oslo, Guillaume, along with his own family, accompanied him as previously scheduled. His position was exceptionally advantageous, since, as the only top aide on the trip, he had the responsibility of retrieving all communications that were being sent to a temporary BND office in a nearby youth hostel. Yet none of the West German security officials had been apprised of the investigation underway and easily struck an amiable relationship with Guillaume. Several times a day he picked up the decoded messages, usually in duplicate, one going to the chancellor, the other into his wardrobe. Among them was a confidential letter from President Richard Nixon to Brandt discussing serious differences with the French regarding NATO strategy.

Opinions differ sharply regarding the fate of the so-called Norway papers. According to Guillaume – who considered this feat his greatest career accomplishment – copies of the documents reached East Berlin via a case officer who had secretly photographed them in the family's hotel room in Halmstad, Sweden, on the return trip to Bonn. As a precaution, prior to leaving Norway, he had given a briefcase to the head of the security detail, maintaining that the sensitivity of the material inside made it inadvisable to be taken in his automobile. In reality, though, it contained souvenirs purchased locally, while the genuine documents remained in his possession in an identical case. Once back in Bonn, he merely switched the cases at an opportune moment. This version, however, was subsequently contradicted by Markus Wolf, who flatly denied ever receiving the Norway papers. He contended that Christel had given them to a female courier at an outdoor café in Bonn. But unable to lose the man closely following her afterwards, the courier had tossed the package into the Rhine.[2] To complicate matters further, Christel later rejected both accounts as inaccurate but gave no explanation herself. The only verifiable fact is the absence of any reference to the Norway papers in the HVA data bank that researchers carefully scrutinized following unification.

The surveillance of both husband and wife continued for the remainder of 1973 with no tangible results. By that point, they had little doubt that their movements were clearly being monitored but still made no request to be exfiltrated. While Wolf ordered them to suspend their intelligence work for an extended period, the actual determination whether to return to the GDR was left in their hands. In retrospect, Wolf regretted his lack of action, noting Guillaume had developed a "certain negligence" because of the unusual ease of his espionage activity heretofore.

Guillaume took a short vacation in southern France the following spring. Although French and West German authorities failed to gather any incriminating material, the fear of the family's imminent departure for the GDR escalated and led to the formulation of Operation TANGO. In the early morning of April 24, 1974, Guillaume and his wife were arrested at their suburban Bonn residence by nearly a dozen armed security officials. Clad only in a bathrobe over his pajamas, he defiantly asserted, "I am a citizen and officer of the GDR. Do respect that." This open admission not only constituted an extremely serious breach of his own espionage training – despite his later rationalizations – but was the only concrete evidence that could guarantee a conviction for the prosecution. Also witnessing this scene was Guillaume's 17-year-old son Pierre, who learned for the first time – to his bitter disillusionment – of his father's double life. A search of the premises produced only a microdot and a wristwatch camera.

Brandt reacted angrily to the news, wondering how the GDR could pursue a policy of détente and simultaneously act in such a blatantly underhand manner. Close political friends urged him not to step down as head of the government. But as the story gained momentum in the press – and included lurid rumors regarding his extramarital affairs – the chancellor decided to resign his office less than two weeks later. In a televised address, he enumerated three reasons: his irresponsibility in allowing Guillaume access to confidential material in Norway; his lack of impartiality toward the GDR as a result of the espionage affair; and his unwillingness to allow his private life to become an object of speculation and potential blackmail. Brandt later simply cited his increasing weariness in office. The following year an independent commission headed by the eminent political scientist Theodor Eschenburg concluded that the Guillaume affair provided the "occasion" for the chancellor's fall from power but should not be considered its root cause. The report further criticized the incompetence of the investigation conducted by West German officials along with the general indifference toward security measures prevalent in the government.

After a lengthy trial in Düsseldorf, Guillaume was sentenced to 13 years in prison for high treason, his wife eight years. As justification, the judge noted that his actions had "endangered the entire Western defense alliance" by giving the other side an undue advantage at the negotiating table. Since spy exchanges had become a routine mechanism in East–West relations, the Guillaumes hoped to be swapped in short order. Given the unusual gravity of the case, however, the West German government displayed little interest when approached (Brandt's successor as chancellor, Helmut Schmidt, wanted him to serve his sentence "to the last day"). At the same time, Guillaume resisted the offer of an early release by divulging the names of other HVA operatives. Finally in October 1981, he was exchanged for eight convicted Western spies (three with life sentences), his wife for six persons the previous March. According to the arrangement, all their names were to be kept confidential.

The return of the Guillaumes to East Berlin was greeted with outward fanfare. Hailed as a "scout for peace," Guillaume received the GDR's highest decoration – the Order of Karl Marx – from Erich Honecker, the country's leader, and was promoted to lieutenant colonel as well. An instructional documentary – *Auftrag erfüllt* (*Mission Accomplished*) – was filmed for future Stasi trainees. The couple took up residence in an idyllic lakeside villa provided by the state, yet their troubled marriage – exacerbated by his own extramarital affairs while in Bonn – soon came asunder. Choosing his mother's surname, their son never found reconciliation with his father.[3] And despite strenuous efforts by the HVA, Pierre's transition to life in a communist state made no headway. His request to return to West Germany was reluctantly granted in 1988, even though his father would have preferred to see him in prison instead.

Guillaume expected to assume a major role in the HVA, but that prospect found no favor with Wolf. The ex-spy's tasks were limited to lecturing several times a week at the Stasi training school in Potsam-Eiche, from which he received an honorary doctorate. His lengthy and tendentious autobiography – ghostwritten with Günter Karau – appeared initially in a limited edition but was released to the public in 1990. Besides burnishing the reputation of the East German service, it sought to place him alongside other famous communist spies such as Richard Sorge and Klaus Fuchs, even though his actual accomplishments seemed meager by comparison.

In a twist of fate, Guillaume was summoned in 1993 to testify at the post-unification trial of Markus Wolf in the same Düsseldorf courtroom where the judge had pronounced the verdict for him and his wife. After a long illness, he died two years later as Günter Bröhl, having remarried and adopted his new wife's name. Christel's death occurred in 2004. From the vantage point of the GDR, the impact of the Guillaume affair was decidedly mixed. On the one hand, it helped to precipitate the removal from office of the most accommodating West German chancellor in the postwar period, causing Wolf to regret what he called the "biggest defeat" of his career – the "equivalent to kicking a football into our own goal." On the other hand, the top GDR leadership deeply feared the growing rapprochement between Moscow and Brandt, as well as the West German chancellor's own popularity among East Germans following an enthusiastic reception during a path-breaking visit to Erfurt in 1970. It was a situation that a state resting on such a precarious foundation could ill afford to tolerate.

Robert Philip Hanssen

One of the most notorious spies in recent American history, Robert Philip Hanssen, often compared himself to Dr. Jekyll and Mr. Hyde. While few would dispute that he displayed a sharply alternating pattern of behavior, it is also one that defies a clear-cut explanation. Hanssen was born on April 18, 1944, in a conservative working-class section of

Chicago. His father, an officer on the city's police force, clashed early on with his only child, while his mother tended to remain quietly in the background. He never tired of complaining about the young Hanssen's shortcomings and even secretly arranged to have him fail his first driving test. Winning a scholarship, he attended Knox College, a small liberal arts institution in Illinois, and majored in chemistry and mathematics. Then, in a seeming act of defiance, Hanssen ignored his father's desire that he become a doctor and chose instead to study dentistry at Northwestern University.

Yet, this career held no appeal, as his postgraduate studies shifted midstream to accounting and information systems with the intention of entering the field of law enforcement – a move that once again incurred his father's disapproval. Hanssen's personal life likewise underwent several major changes. In marrying Bernadette (Bonnie) Wauck, whose family was staunchly Catholic, he decided to abandon his own Protestant faith and convert, even taking an extra step and joining the ultra-orthodox lay order, Opus Dei. He had initially hoped to work for the National Security Agency, but his application was rejected. Nevertheless, in 1972, with an MBA in hand, Hanssen found a position with the Chicago police only months after his father had retired from the force. The unit to which he was assigned – the undercover C-5 – had the special task of investigating police corruption, often through carefully staged sting operations. His own ambitions, however, were considerably higher, prompting him three years later to seek out the FBI for employment and, once accepted, to begin a new stage in his life as a special agent.

Following training in Quantico, Virginia – where he excelled in the classroom and at the shooting range but was found deficient in physical activity – Hanssen was assigned briefly to the field office in Indianapolis, then to the one in New York City. Although his initial duties involved mostly basic accounting procedures, a fresh assignment in March 1979 placed him squarely in the intelligence division. He was to assist in creating a new classified national counterintelligence database for the FBI. That gave him a comprehensive overview of Soviet intelligence officers working for both the KGB and the GRU – an especially extensive network because of numerous sites in Manhattan such as the United Nations.

Within a matter of months, Hanssen next proceeded to the local branch office of Amtorg, the Soviet commercial trading agency, and offered to sell his services to the GRU. Altogether three separate deliveries were made through encoded radio transmissions and one-time pads, an unbreakable cipher system favored by the Soviets. This information included not just the FBI lists of Eastern bloc intelligence officers but the revelation that one in the employ of the GRU, Dimitri Fedorovich

Polyakov, had been a highly prized CIA asset (code name TOPHAT) for the past 17 years. A new complication arose when Hanssen's wife accidentally stumbled upon her husband's covert activity in the couple's basement. Admitting that confidential matter was being sold to the Soviets yet falsely downplaying its significance, he agreed to see an Opus Dei priest familiar to Bonnie and her family. After carefully contemplating Hanssen's confession, he ended up recommending that nothing be reported to the authorities but that the payments received be distributed to a worthy charity.

The following phase of Hanssen's career began with his transfer to FBI headquarters in Washington, DC, in early 1981. There, working with the euphemistically named Dedicated Technical Program, he found increased exposure to confidential information and sophisticated surveillance methods. Hanssen's technical knowledge impressed his superiors – he soon became one of the bureau's experts in the use of polygraphs – while many colleagues felt rebuffed by his aloof, if not arrogant, manner. Another assignment in the budget unit further added to his store of knowledge, since, as a routine matter, he had access to the full range of the FBI's planned intelligence and counterintelligence operations that would require Congressional funding. Two years later, a transfer across the hall brought him into the Soviet analytical office formally designated as CI-3A. In this capacity, Hanssen could learn with greater specificity how the agency employed double agents and also detected enemy penetrations of the US government.

The year 1985 turned out to be pivotal in several respects. On the national scene, it saw the arrest and ultimate conviction of nearly a dozen important spies, including Richard Miller, the first FBI agent ever found guilty of espionage. Hanssen, doubtlessly aware of the heightened level of surveillance and publicity but apparently relishing the challenge it posed, decided to resume his role as a double agent with the other major Soviet organ, the KGB. While in the process of moving back to the New York City area for his second tour, he mailed a letter from Maryland addressed to Viktor M. Degtyar, a KGB officer in Alexandria, Virginia, who was instructed to convey the enclosed envelope to Victor Cherkashin, the KGB chief of counterintelligence at the Soviet embassy. Suggesting in return the payment of US$100,000, the typed unsigned letter promised a box of classified documents to be delivered to Degtyar and, as a gesture to establish Hanssen's *bona fides*, named three KGB members who had been recruited by the Americans.

Once the box was sent, Hanssen sent a follow-up letter from New York to Degtyar's address with detailed instructions for conveying the money to him. It was to be left in a plastic garbage bag under a wooden footbridge in Nottoway Park in Fairfax County, Virginia. Signals were to be exchanged using white adhesive tape on a nearby "pedestrian crossing" signpost. This dead drop – simply codenamed PARK by the KGB – turned out to be Hanssen's favorite site and was utilized 17 times during the next four years. Although the money he received had been halved by the KGB, it prompted no complaint from him, as his next letter began with a straightforward expression of esteem for Cherkashin's work. Besides telling of his access to highly confidential NSA materials, he made his first request for an escape plan, showing he had no illusions about the implicit dangers presented by this new relationship.

To his coworkers at the FBI, Hanssen gave no indication in his daily performance of a diminished commitment to thwart Soviet influence in the United States. Yet, his tasks in New York – supervising a nondescript surveillance squad – provided little satisfaction and caused him to end his tour prematurely and return to Washington, DC, which, of course, put him in much closer proximity to his preferred dead drop. In a moment of unusual irony, his superiors then selected him to head a team that was to comb the FBI's vast counterintelligence files with the objective of finding any traitors within the organization. Certainly his own immunity from detection was thereby immeasurably enhanced, as he could easily sweep aside any incriminating evidence, however minor in nature. Once completed, this top-secret report replete with the identity of the individual sources also found its way to Moscow.

In the meantime, his dealings with the KGB began to manifest several decidedly atypical characteristics. Initially using the pseudonym "Ramon Garcia," Hanssen studiously avoided divulging his real name. It remains a debated question whether the KGB ever learned it prior to his eventual exposure; at least it does not appear in the official dossier later obtained by the FBI.[4] When the KGB followed its standard procedure with new agents and requested a meeting outside the country – possibly in Europe or South America – Hanssen flatly refused and threatened to abort the relationship. In another odd twist, he insisted on making the selection of the dead drop himself. That it was located near his home and used multiple times further contradicted basic spycraft practice. He reasoned, however, that a pattern that deviated so much from the norm had less potential of arousing the suspicions of the FBI. Having already obtained a bounty of documents and other valuable information, the KGB quietly suppressed any objections. In fact, its chairman at the time, Vladimir Kryuchkov, conveyed his personal regards on more than one occasion.

Despite his increasing wealth – in excess of US$400,000 by 1990 – the family lived modestly, and he continued to drive a late model car to

66

work. Attending mass every morning, Hanssen likewise appeared attentive to his wife and six children. But beneath his outwardly conventional domestic life lurked some strange aberrations. Hanssen's attraction to strip clubs, for instance, led him to befriend a number of women performers and to bestow expensive gifts to one in particular. They included not just expensive jewelry and a used Mercedes sedan but a roundtrip to Hong Kong – each on separate flights and with separate hotel accommodations – as sex never became a motivating factor during their extended contact. Presumably he wanted to guide her to a more religious and respectable middle-class lifestyle, even though these attempts eventually failed with her subsequent arrest and conviction for selling crack cocaine. Even harder to explain is Hanssen's exploitation of his own wife. Unknown to Bonnie, he took much pleasure in posting nude pictures of her on the internet accompanied by a salacious commentary. In addition, for his closest friend dating from his high school days, a closed-circuit video hookup to the basement was installed that allowed him to view the couple's live lovemaking in the upstairs bedroom.

Another family member – Mark Wauck, Hanssen's brother-in-law – entered the picture and came to play a potentially decisive role. By coincidence, Wauck had joined the FBI only two years after Hanssen, and over time, the two men developed a certain professional rapport. Yet, some troubling signs began to accumulate, especially when Wauck learned that a large sum of money had been left lying on his sister's bedroom dresser. While he later recalled telling a supervisor in Chicago of his suspicions and urging an investigation of his brother-in-law, no official corroboration of his story exists. The key point is that no alert ever reached the main headquarters in Washington, thus allowing Hanssen another decade to practice his espionage.

What Hanssen succeeded in delivering to the KGB seems astonishing in retrospect. Just a brief glimpse at the 6,000-page inventory reveals a broad range of confidential topics often extending beyond the scope of the FBI–CIA wiretaps and recruitment attempts in Moscow, intelligence sources of US allies, domestic surveillance operations, the electronic intercepts of the NSA, and the status of nuclear and missile technology in both countries. When the new Soviet embassy complex was under construction at Mount Alto in Washington, DC, Hanssen gave timely warning of Operation MONOPOLY – the technologically sophisticated secret tunnel that the FBI was simultaneously burrowing under the building for purposes of eavesdropping at a cost of nearly US$1 billion. Furthermore, by the spring of 1990, the KGB had learned the identity of numerous human sources. As a consequence of Hanssen's betrayal, three of these individuals were executed.

With the Soviet Union facing imminent collapse the following year, the KGB took pains to reassure its prized asset of his continuing worth, emphasizing his "superb sense of humor" and "sharp-as-a-razor mind."[5] By letting him believe that he was the controlling partner, the Soviet operatives also showed the degree to which they understood Hanssen's deep-set psychological needs. Still, the transition of the KGB to the new Russian service, the SVR, posed some acute dangers, particularly given the stream of former Soviet intelligence personnel who chose to defect to the CIA. After fulfilling his last assignment in mid-December 1991, Hanssen, offering no explanation, terminated all contact with his handlers.

This hiatus lasted for less than two years. Spurred by curiosity about the fate of his previous information, he approached a GRU officer in an apartment house garage with a bundle of documents and identified himself as "Ramon Garcia." This rash encounter – indicative of his increasing mental fragility – came to naught, as the Russians suspected a sting operation by US authorities. Another six years passed before financial worries caused Hanssen to establish a new arrangement with a very receptive SVR. While he took some solace in not finding any suspicion pointing in his direction on the FBI's confidential database of ongoing investigations – and that no polygraph test had ever been administered – the search for a mole had, in fact, intensified. Brian Kelley, a veteran CIA counterintelligence officer bearing numerous resemblances to Hanssen, was subjected to FBI surveillance for three years, interrogated, and then placed on extended administrative leave before the true facts came to light.

On February 18, 2001, Hanssen was arrested while making a dead drop delivery in Foxstone Park near his home in suburban northern Virginia. By finally locating a cooperative former KGB and SVR officer through Operation BUCKLURE – and paying him the exceptional sum of U$7 million – the FBI had succeeded in obtaining Hanssen's complete Moscow dossier and was in a position to ascertain the real "Ramon Garcia" with little difficulty. His first remark – "What took you so long?" – indicated that fatigue had taken its toll and that this moment had been clearly anticipated. As he was being driven away, the agents enumerated some of the voluminous evidence such as photographs, letters, and a secretly taped telephone conversation in 1986 with a KGB operative.

Because a credible defense seemed almost futile from the outset, Hanssen decided to accept a plea bargain – an arrangement much preferred by both the FBI and CIA whose first priority was obtaining a full and accurate damage assessment. In addition, a public trial would have probably forced the exposure of the FBI's secret source along with other confidential matters. After pleading guilty to 13 counts of espionage, Hanssen was given a life sentence with no possibility of parole. All of his payments – US$1.4 million in total – were forfeited, and he could not benefit from any future book, film, or other publicity. His debriefing was to continue for the next six months.

Caught completely by surprise by the revelations that emerged, his wife fully cooperated with officials. Despite her intense anger regarding his exploitation of her, she visited him in the nearby detention center and decided not to seek an annulment but to keep her marriage vows intact. A portion of his regular pension – the equivalent of a survivor benefit – was allotted to her as compensation. The US government also expelled 50 Russian diplomats as a symbolic protest, which prompted a similar retaliatory move by authorities in Moscow.

The mystery lingers regarding the wellsprings of Hanssen's treachery. Former CIA Director James Woolsey stressed the "truly odd" nature of the case, as Hanssen eludes all of the previously known categories of spies. Money appears to have played only a limited role. Given the extraordinary value of his deliveries, a significantly higher price could have been exacted from the Soviets, but he never negotiated a larger sum. Rather, the payments served, in his mind, as reassurance that he was a good provider for his family and not a failure.

Many of his FBI colleagues described Hanssen as a quiet introvert outside the inner circle and never a leader. Nicknamed "the mortician" for his dark suits and cheerless manner, he remained aloof from the daily office banter. And, although known for his computer skills, he had never been involved in a recruitment or successful espionage case. Yet, he nurtured the illusion of being a top-flight spy and esteemed the professionalism of the KGB as "the only enemy worth fighting." His feeling of superiority, already evident in his outward manner, must have been enhanced by believing that he knew more about the overall situation than anyone in the bureau or the KGB. Sensing his loneliness without knowing his actual identity, the latter also offered him the friendship and recognition that he had not found elsewhere. The thrill of living on the edge played a role as well. At the same time, according to a psychiatrist engaged by Hanssen's defense attorney, his religious beliefs had a genuine core and did not serve as camouflage for his espionage. "He believes his religion requires him to atone for what he has done and to suffer – he has used the term mortification – to come back to the proper relationship with God."[6]

As a result of the case, the FBI's image in the public mind suffered a major blow, underscored by a subsequent investigation by the US Justice Department. Noting that "from the outset the FBI was focused on the wrong suspect at the wrong agency," it called for significant, long overdue reforms – "a wholesale change in mindset and approach to internal security."[7] By contrast, officials in Moscow were able to celebrate what former KGB general Oleg Kalugin called "one of the greatest feats of Russian intelligence." What Hanssen provided, as his handler noted afterward, went to "the heart of Washington's intelligence infrastructure."[8] As late as 2010, the Russians expressed their desire to obtain Hanssen in a spy swap – an unprecedented move since never before had they wanted their American recruits to be included in such an exchange. Yet in actuality – with this unstated admission of Hanssen's continuing value to Russian intelligence – his chances of ever being released from prison were diminished even further.

Ryszard Kuklinski

Ryszard Kuklinski's induction into the brutal power politics that has characterized modern Polish history occurred at an early age. Born in Warsaw to working-class Catholic parents on June 13, 1930, he witnessed the city's invasion by German forces with the outbreak of World War II. His response to the terror-filled occupation that followed was to try to join the Home Army, a large underground resistance organization directed by the exile government in London; but deemed too young, he found his participation denied. Soon thereafter, his family's apartment became the site of a bloody Gestapo interrogation of his father, who subsequently perished in the Sachsenhausen-Oranienburg concentration camps outside Berlin. Kuklinski and several other boys naively believed that they could turn a Nazi recruiting campaign for Polish workers to their advantage, but the unintended outcome was 18 months of forced labor in German wartime factories.

The end of the war brought little stability to his life. After searching in vain for his father in the environs of Berlin, Kuklinski moved to Wroclaw and found a job as a night watchman in a soap factory, which enabled him to pursue his studies during the day. Then, in September 1947, he fulfilled his ardent childhood desire and enlisted in the Polish Army, hoping that its current domination by the Red Army would prove to be only a temporary phenomenon. Yet during the next three years in officers' school, Soviet influence made itself felt on nearly every level – from the teaching staff to the format of the drills and the design of the uniforms. A stellar student at the top of his class, he nevertheless felt constrained to join the Communist Party. It took, however, only an anti-Soviet joke told to a classmate just months before his graduation to bring about his expulsion from both the party and the school. Reduced to the status of an ordinary soldier serving in a regiment near Poznan for the next two years, Kuklinski filed an appeal that eventually led to his reinstatement at the school, although his promotion to warrant officer noticeably fell below the rank of full officer.

Still, his fortunes continued to rise. Advanced military studies near Warsaw along with his marriage were quickly followed by a promotion to captain and the position as chief of staff to a coastal defense battalion. A significant step in Kuklinski's career next resulted from his superior performance at the General Staff Academy, for upon graduation in 1963, having attained the rank of major, he received an appointment to the General Staff in Warsaw. His expertise regarding the military exercises conducted by Poland with other members of the Warsaw Pact made him the leading authority on the subject in short order.

The dominant role played by Poland within the Warsaw Pact should be noted as well. It served as the headquarters for the Soviet Union's Western Theater of Operations, and it could boast of the third largest army in Europe after the USSR and the Federal Republic of Germany (and the second largest within the Warsaw Pact). Polish factories produced a variety of war-related goods – from steel, munitions, and ships to precision instruments for the Soviet space program. The Red Army also maintained a strong presence and, not insignificantly, kept a secret stockpile of nuclear weapons in the country.

As his access to confidential information increased, Kuklinski grew deeply troubled by the offensive nature of the planned strategy. A first wave containing 600,000 Polish troops was to sweep into the Federal Republic of Germany, Denmark, and the Low Countries; then, within two days, Western Europe would witness an even more massive assault by at least two million soldiers coming from positions inside the Soviet Union. Kuklinski further observed the so-called "training exercise" immediately prior to Operation DANUBE – the 1968 Warsaw Pact invasion of Czechoslovakia that brought an end to the reform aspirations of the Prague Spring. That afterwards so many of his colleagues – especially Defense Minister Wojciech Jaruzelski – hailed Polish participation in the military crackdown only added to his profound disenchantment. Likewise, leaving an indelible imprint two years later was the armed suppression of Polish shipyard workers – resulting in nearly four dozen fatalities – by his country's own soldiers.

But most troubling of all was his knowledge that military planners expected NATO to react to an invasion by launching tactical nuclear weapons aimed at the second troop wave just as it was crossing Poland. Envisioning his homeland as the principal target of even more deadly warfare than in the recent past prompted Kuklinski to take bold action himself. An accomplished sailor, he used the pretext of heading an official surveillance cruise through Western European waterways on a small yacht in order to mail a letter from Wilhelmshaven, Germany, to the US military attaché in Bonn. His request for a meeting with a person of similar rank was ultimately forwarded to Carl Gerhardt, the new CIA chief of station in Warsaw.

Although the first attempts to establish personal contact failed, so determined was Kuklinski that he proceeded to improvise a darkroom inside his bathroom and began photographing whatever he possibly could – secret documents from his workplace as well as scenes from his walks and weekend sailing trips. On a late evening in mid-December 1972, an exchange between the two men finally took place in a Warsaw cemetery, causing CIA officials at Langley to react with exceeding satisfaction to the 18 rolls of film relayed to them via diplomatic pouch. Besides a code name (GULL) and a pseudonym ("Jack Strong"), Kuklinski received two technologically advanced cameras and special water-soluble writing paper for messages. In addition, extremely tight security restrictions surrounded this new asset, such as attaching the names of other sources to his classified information before its wider circulation. A final step was to assign him a case officer, Jack Forden (pseudonym "Daniel"), who was almost identical in age and fluent in Polish from his earlier posting in the country.

Their first substantive meeting took place at a Hamburg safe house – during another of Kuklinski's yacht trips – where Forden revealed the CIA connection for the first time, explaining that his organization was the one best equipped to handle a clandestine relationship of this nature. He found himself impressed by Kuklinski's modest, direct manner and his keen memory for detail. Far from regarding himself a traitor, the Polish officer stressed how he wanted to avenge those who had brought his country into such dire straits and that the United States represented not just the other superpower but the most viable force for the advancement of human freedom. Discussion also centered on the issue of personal safety, as he explained that his wife and two sons had purposely been kept ignorant of his undertaking for fear that they might inadvertently – or under pressure – make an incriminating remark.

Given his desire to supply the Americans with as much confidential material as possible – especially those items that had been specifically requested – it is hardly surprising that Kuklinski veered dangerously close to being detected more than once. The most harrowing instance took place one evening in early September 1974. Immediately after making what Forden called a "moving car delivery" (packages are quickly exchanged through the passenger window while the US embassy automobile is momentarily stopped), a surveillance vehicle belonging to the SB, the Polish secret police, spotted Kuklinski on foot in its headlights, and a long labyrinthine chase ensued through the streets of Warsaw and into its immediate suburbs. Although he methodically managed to elude the security personnel, the incident left him in a genuine quandary and more anxious than ever about his personal safety. After reviewing his detailed report, his CIA handlers recommended that he suspend his activities temporarily and destroy his photographic equipment and message pads. That advice, however, went unheeded, probably because he felt a measure of reassurance when his superiors re-selected him to attend the prestigious Vorshilov Academy in Moscow for an abbreviated two-month course.

As time passed, each side could claim a high degree of satisfaction with Kuklinski's performance. Noting that he had provided roughly 20,000 pages of "secret" and "top secret" material during the first five years of their association, both Forden and others in the CIA Soviet Division urged that he be awarded the Distinguished Intelligence Medal, the agency's highest honor normally reserved for its own personnel. No asset within the Soviet bloc, in their view, could match his productivity in terms of quantity or quality.[9] Their recommendation, though, was not realized until Kuklinski's later arrival in the United States. Meanwhile, he became the recipient of two Polish commendations: the Amor Patriae Supreme Lex and the Cavalier's Cross of the Order of the Rebirth of Poland, the latter accompanied by a formal ceremony held on Army Day. A new appointment in April 1977 – chief of the First Department for Strategic Defense Planning – gave him access to even more valuable classified information and automatically placed him on three critical Warsaw Pact committees.

Despite the exceptional materials that Kuklinski was able to convey – notably the Warsaw Pact's comprehensive four-year weapons development plans – concerns about his safety continued to mount. Not only did a misplaced canister of film cause him to suspend his activity and dispose of his equipment temporarily – this time following the CIA's advice – but the agency never ceased refining its exfiltration plan for him and his family in case of an emergency. Aware that Soviet bloc counterintelligence suspected a major leak, the agency also cautioned Kuklinski about an established KGB technique of using a slightly altered test document as a means of determining whether it had been passed on to the West. Efforts, too, were made to accelerate communications between Kuklinski and the US embassy through a new electronic transmitting device and not rely on the normal chalk mark signals on various prearranged objects.

The rise of the independent labor union Solidarity (*Solidarnosc*) and the response of the communist regime presented new complications for Kuklinski. As secret preparations for the suppression of Solidarity and the imposition of martial law began, he was requested to oversee a small planning group regarding the military's involvement. Although such a task ran completely counter to his unbounded admiration for the growing movement and its leader Lech Wałesa, it nevertheless offered the possibility of exerting some influence on events and keeping the CIA informed of the rapidly evolving situation. Indeed, during this tense period, Kuklinski's reports functioned as a prime inside source for leading policymakers in the US government; his information, often mixed with other sources, was distributed to some 20 persons and usually attributed to "an allegedly reliable Polish senior military official." Yet, in the fall of 1981 – through a source stationed in Rome – the SB learned that the CIA had obtained a copy of the latest version of the martial-law plans. Because only a small number of Polish officials had been privy to this document, Kuklinski realized – upon being told of the leak by one of his superiors – that suspicion would rapidly turn to him.

While the agency had responded reluctantly to his repeated request and supplied him with a cyanide pill concealed in a fountain pen, he rejected suicide at this juncture in favor of attempting to flee the country with his family. Besides notifying his handlers of his extreme predicament, he systematically destroyed all of the materials in his possession that might prove incriminating if discovered. The CIA's exfiltration plan consisted basically of two parts: bringing the entire family into the US embassy without attracting attention; and then transporting them across the border into Western Europe and eventually to the United States. Heavy SB surveillance twice delayed the first part, but a couple based at the Warsaw station managed to pick up the family one evening at a locale named Skron and keep them concealed in the car during the trip back to the embassy. They were next assisted into a large packing carton placed in the rear of a van bearing US diplomatic plates. A short delay occurred at the Polish border with East Germany, but the van appeared to be making a routine delivery to a West Berlin military base and thus reached its destination without incident. Flown first to Frankfurt am Main, the family secretly arrived in the United States in December 1981 and were taken directly to a safe house in Virginia.

The public revelation of Kuklinski's identity came – oddly enough – in June 1986 through an initiative of Jaruzelski's martial-law regime, the Military Council of National Salvation. Anxious to discredit the Reagan administration in light of its covert aid to Solidarity, Jerzy Urban, the regime's combative press spokesman, arranged for an exclusive interview with a leading reporter for the *Washington Post*. The resulting front-page story told of a CIA agent working inside the military staff who had been exfiltrated with his family to the United States and subsequently sentenced to death in absentia by a Polish military court. According to Urban, because Kuklinski had participated in drafting the operational blueprint for martial law, the CIA possessed advance warning of the impending crackdown, but the Reagan administration, in an act of sheer betrayal, withheld this information from its so-called allies in Solidarity. Presumably such a warning would have rendered the imposition of martial law impossible. At a press conference two days later, Urban went even further by asserting that the US president had intentionally hoped to provoke "a bloodbath of European proportions" in order to advance his country's "imperialist" agenda.[10] In reality, however, Kuklinski's knowledge was restricted to a contingency plan with no guarantee of implementation, while most Washington policy-makers and intelligence analysts, aware of increased military maneuvers in the region, seemed transfixed by the threat of a Soviet invasion.

The following year, Kuklinski injected himself into the simmering debate. In a lengthy interview with *Kultura*, a respected Polish émigré journal published in Paris, he described his motivation along with details of his clandestine activity just prior to the advent of martial law.[11] Moreover, he contended that the communist regime had sought to crush Solidarity from the outset, having formulated the first plans for martial law much earlier than generally assumed, and that the negotiations that had taken place with the opposition were a mere smokescreen. Most provocative of all was Kuklinski's response to the question of whether Jaruzelski had, in fact, rescued the nation from a worse fate. He felt convinced that both a Soviet invasion and martial law could have been averted by a bolder, less subservient Polish leadership. As a result, a heated controversy quickly ensued that pitted the colonel against the general and that was to cause a deep fissure to develop in the country.

With the fall of the communist regime and the overwhelming election of Lech Wałesa as president in December 1990, the Kuklinski case entered a new phase. Although his death sentence was commuted to 25 years in prison and loss of civil rights as part of a general political amnesty, no additional remedial action by the new government was deemed appropriate. An appeal to Wałesa by Zbigniew Brzezinski, the former US national security advisor and Kuklinski's staunchest advocate in the West, had no impact at all. (Upon meeting Kuklinski in Washington, Brzezinski greeted him with the Polish phrase used to confer honors on a soldier: "*Pan sie dobrze Polsce zasluzyl!* [You have served Poland well!]") As more details about his undercover career came to light – specifically the actual length of his espionage activity and his means of escape – voices on both sides grew increasingly adamant. Jaroslaw Kacynski, head of the center-right Center Alliance Party, challenged Wałesa to pardon Kuklinski or make his objections publicly known. Among those still unforgiving was General Czelaw Kiszczak, the interior minister during the martial law period, who found his acts an outright betrayal of the Polish state. Jaruzelski, then in retirement, expressed his "painful" personal disappointment in the colonel and suggested that blackmail by the CIA might well have been the precipitating factor.

Whereas Wałesa remained ambivalent, maintaining that the matter needed "time and preparation," Kuklinski firmly rejected any halfway measures such as clemency or a pardon and demanded full exoneration. Just as his former neighbors in the Rajcow Street housing cooperative took opposite sides in the matter, so, too, national public opinion polls registered a stark divergence of views. One representative survey taken in mid-November 1996 found 27 percent of Poles considering him a traitor, 21 percent a patriot.

Two related developments should be noted as well. One was the case of Marian Zacharski, a Polish intelligence officer who became known as the "Silicon Valley spy" because of his success acquiring American technological secrets. Although arrested in 1981 and given a life sentence, he was later included in one of the periodic East–West spy swaps and returned to Poland. In 1994, upon hearing that Zacharski had been selected to head the civilian intelligence branch of the Office of State Protection, US officials voiced their objections, causing the Polish government to retreat and withdraw the appointment. For some Poles, this action of the United States seemed to constitute not only an unwanted intrusion into their domestic affairs but a glaring double-standard in the treatment of former Cold War spies. The other key factor concerned Poland's overriding desire to become a member of NATO. In the opinion of Richard Davies, a former US ambassador to Poland, it was a "grotesque irony" to witness "the one Pole who risked his life to assist NATO before 1989 called a traitor and subject to incarceration, while the leaders of today's Poland pride themselves on their participation in NATO exercises and press for full membership in the organization."[12] Brzezinski summed up the situation by simply calling Kuklinski "the first Polish officer of NATO."

In March 1995, the country's Supreme Court took a significant step in Kuklinski's rehabilitation. Overcoming the rather strange alliance between a group of communist-era generals still in service and certain ex-Solidarity activists, the acting chief justice called on the country's highest military court to undertake an extraordinary review of the case.

The five judges, however, rendered only a half-hearted verdict, lifting Kuklinski's conviction and sentence while calling for further investigation by the military prosecutors. In the presence of Brzezinski and the Polish ambassador to the United States, Jerzy Kozminski, they met with Kuklinski in Washington for an extended interrogation regarding the two formal allegations: desertion and flight and passing classified information to NATO. Finally, when his exoneration was announced in September 1997 – it referred to his acting under "conditions of higher necessity" – he expressed relief, noting that it had "symbolic rather than practical meaning for me." The following spring saw his return to Poland – a ten-day visit to six cities, including Kraców, which had earlier extended honorary citizenship to him. He received a warm reception as well as numerous awards throughout his tour, even though the national debate about patriotism and duty had by no means dissipated. Adam Michnik, the prominent editor of *Gazeta Wyborcza* and former political prisoner during the martial-law period, wrote that he saw no heroism in Kuklinski's behavior but rather an act of subservience to the United States. Wałesa, too, kept his distance and would only meet with him if so requested. By contrast, he remained unknown to the wider American public despite being the first foreign recipient of the CIA's Distinguished Intelligence Medal.

After a fatal stroke in 2004, Kuklinski's ashes were flown from Florida back to Warsaw for burial in the honor row of the Powązki military cemetery. Those of his older son were also returned (both brothers had died in separate mysterious and unclarified accidents – one in an automobile collision, the other lost at sea). While thousands of Poles and ranking officials attended the ceremony, the government, tellingly, chose not to send an official representative.

Notes

1 Hubertus Knabe, "Der Kanzleramtspion," in Wolfgang Krieger (Ed.), *Geheimdienste in der Weltgeschichte: Spionage und verdeckte Aktionen von der Antike bis zur Gegenwart* (Munich: C. H. Beck, 2003), 218.
2 Markus Wolf (with Anne McElvoy), *Man Without a Face: The Autobiography of Communism's Greatest Spymaster* (New York, NY: Times Books, 1997), 159–160.
3 See Pierre Boom (with Gerhard Haase-Hindenburg), *Der fremde Vater: Der Sohn des Kanzlerspions Guillaume erinnert sich* (Berlin: Aufbau Verlag, 2004).
4 See Victor Cherkashin (with Gregory Feifer), *Spy Handler: Memoir of a KGB Officer* (New York, NY: Basic Books, 2005), 240.
5 Cited by David Wise, *Spy: The Inside Story of How the FBI's Robert Hanssen Betrayed America* (New York, NY: Random House, 2002), 137.
6 Cited by Wise, *Spy*, 240.

7 An unclassified executive summary can be found at http://www.justice.gov/ oig/special/0308/index.htm.
8 Cherkashin, *Spy Handler*, 246.
9 Eighty-two documents released by the CIA in December 2008 can be found at http://www.wilsoncenter.org/article/new-kuklinski-documents-martial-law-poland-released.
10 Cited by Benjamin B. Fischer, "Entangled in History: The Vilification and Vindication of Colonel Kuklinski," *Studies in Intelligence* (Summer 2000), 9, unclassified edition, 21.
11 Translated and reprinted as "The Crushing of Solidarity," *Orbis*, 32(1) (Winter 1988), 5–31.
12 Cited by Benjamin Weiser, *A Secret Life: The Polish Officer, His Covert Mission, and the Price He Paid to Save His Country* (New York, NY: Public Affairs, 2004), 312.

6   Espionage in Fiction and Film

A history of Cold War espionage would be incomplete without making a short side excursion and examining how it entered the popular imagination through the medium of fiction, movies, and television. In some instances, the images and terminology created began to take on a life of their own. From the perspective of literary history, the spy novel is a relatively recent genre, having originated in Britain during the waning years of the nineteenth century. As rivalries among the great powers were growing ever more pronounced, a number of authors began to detect sinister, less visible forces at work. The public spectacle of the Dreyfus Affair in France should not be forgotten either, as it was sparked by the betrayal of French military secrets to the Germans and then grew to a protracted nation-wide scandal. For the English, fear of an invasion from the continent, while by no means lacking prior precedents, assumed a heightened intensity, fueled by the shrill warnings of a mass-circulation press.

Published in 1903, an early classic by Erskine Childers – *The Riddle of the Sands*, or "a yachting story, with a purpose" in his words – sought to awaken the British public to the country's vulnerability to Germany's secret designs, which, in this case, were abetted by a turncoat former Royal Navy officer. A far more prolific and melodramatic writer, William Le Queux (an Englishman, despite his surname), likewise popularized the German threat, particularly in *Spies of the Kaiser* by postulating the existence of a network of 5,000 spies preparing the way for an invasion. The most important author to emerge during World War I was John Buchan, whose fictional clubland secret agent Richard Hannay, racing against time, sought to thwart an international conspiracy in *The Thirty-Nine Steps*.

For all their stylistic differences, this initial generation of spy writers shared a number of notable characteristics. Basically gifted amateurs, their heroes were motivated in the first instance by their unflinching loyalty to England in the face of threats from abroad. One finds nothing devious in these characters or overly convoluted in the action-oriented fast-moving plots that unfold. Doubts about the rightness of their cause never entered the realm of possibility. A major shift in motivation, however, occurred in the aftermath of World War I – one seen with particular clarity in W. Somerset Maugham's influential *Ashenden* appearing in 1928. Drawing upon his own wartime experiences as an intelligence officer in Switzerland and Russia, he quickly dispelled the image of the idealistic Edwardian gentleman-agent in favor of a disenchanted government employee mired in a career of boredom, routine, and seeming moral indifference.

Deeply indebted to Maugham, Eric Ambler – the preeminent spy writer of the 1930s – carried this astringent realism forward in such works as *The Mask of Dimitrios* (*A Coffin for Dimitrios* in the United States) and *Journey into Fear*. Preferring to focus on those individuals uprooted by recent social and political turmoil in Europe and forced to live principally by their own wits, Ambler, in addition, displayed a painstaking concern for technical and historical accuracy, which helped to establish his high reputation among intelligence professionals on both sides of the Atlantic. Sharing his somber mood – and left-wing, anticapitalist sympathies – was another prominent writer, Graham Greene, who tried his hand at a spy novel in 1939, *The Confidence Man*, set against the backdrop of the Spanish Civil War. Mention should also be made of two women novelists making a first appearance in this period: Marte McKenna, a spy herself for the British in her native Belgium during World War I; and Helen McInnes, a Scottish transplant to the United States who, beginning with *Assignment in Brittany* in 1942, was to become known as the "queen of the spy novel" and the favorite writer of at least three directors of the Central Intelligence Agency.

The Cold War ushered in a new expanded era of spy fiction – one less defined by its homogeneity than by its sheer diversity. Invariably the first author who comes to mind is Ian Fleming. No one, however, anticipated the fictional phenomenon that was in the making when he began typing his first James Bond novel at his Jamaican retreat in February 1952. Little in his background had pointed to a clear career path. Descended from a wealthy and landed Anglo-Scottish family, Fleming left the Royal Military College at Sandhurst before graduating and later fell short of acceptance by the Foreign Office. He then worked brief stints as a stockbroker and merchant banker before becoming a writer and manager for the *Sunday Times* after the war.

The experience that left the deepest impression had occurred during the war while serving as an aide to the Director of Naval Intelligence, Rear Admiral John Henry Godfrey. His responsibilities extended into a variety of fields – propaganda, press relations, even devising some espionage schemes of his own such as scuttling cement barges in the

Danube River to disrupt German shipping and luring enemy agents to a trap set in Monte Carlo. One notable plan did find realization – the creation of a skilled commando group (30 Assault Unit) that collected intelligence in advance of the principal British forces. Godfrey later recalled that no operational secrets had been withheld from Fleming. On a trip to Washington, DC, in May 1941, he met with William Donovan – who was then soliciting advice for what became the OSS – and was asked to write a 70-page memorandum outlining what a postwar US intelligence agency ought to encompass.

A popular misconception holds that the James Bond novels represent little more than an escapist fantasy filled with acute danger and sybaritic pleasures. Yet, a closer comparison of these works with events known to the author reveal many striking parallels. Fleming once stated that "my plots are fantastic, while often being based on truth. They go wildly beyond the probable, but not, I think, beyond the possible."[1] The planned assassination of Bond in *Casino Royale* distinctly echoes a similar episode in 1942 – the failed attempt on the life of Franz von Papen, the former spymaster and then ambassador to Turkey, by Bulgarians acting as Soviet agents and committing suicide afterward. Likewise, in all probability, the wartime exploits of an Italian unit of elite navy frogmen who attacked Allied ships off the Gibraltar coast – "the greatest piece of effrontery in the underwater war,"[2] according to Fleming – formed the basis of daring aquatic sequences in *Thunderball* and *Live and Let Die*. Foreign locales were routinely scouted in advance and retained their authenticity in print.

The names of various characters and objects can often be traced to a counterpart in Fleming's life as well. Anyone in his social circle (or tangentially linked to it) or embedded in his memory could easily be appropriated, either in whole or in part. Two schoolmates from Eton found their family names attached to arch villains Hugo Drax in *Moonraker* and Ernst Stavro Blofield in *You Only Live Twice*. A New York lawyer friend, Ernie Cuneo, was transformed into Ernie Cureo, a knowledgeable Las Vegas taxi driver and undercover CIA agent in *Diamonds Are Forever*. Ernö Goldfinger, a well-known modernist architect, strenuously objected to the use of his surname and threatened to halt publication of the novel but to no avail. In a short story appearing posthumously, a man-eating octopus was dubbed Octopussy after a small boat of that name presented to him by a later lover, Blanche Blackwell. In *Dr. No*, her given name was transferred to an aged guano-collecting tanker.

So-called Bondologists have advanced a number of theories regarding the central character. The most plausible explanation – one confirmed by Fleming himself – is that his eye happened to land on a book in his library in Jamaica entitled *Field Guide to Birds of the West Indies* by James Bond, a distinguished American ornithologist. Yet other possibilities exist, such as a minor character in a 1934 Agatha Christie short story or a church in Toronto, St. James Bond, which he might have seen during a wartime visit to Canada. More important was Fleming's intent, as he desired something "brief, unromantic, Anglo-Saxon, and yet very masculine." After refusing to accept a knighthood in *The Man with the Golden Gun*, Bond reflected for a moment: "No middle name. No hyphen. A quiet, dull anonymous name." The code name 007 appears to derive from the wartime intelligence practice of attaching a double zero to all highly classified documents; the "rare double-O prefix," as noted in *Goldfinger*, now meant "the licence to kill in the Secret Service."

To what extent did the invention of Bond mirror Fleming's own life? While certain physical resemblances between the two men existed, there were other credible contenders, including his father and older brother and a naval intelligence officer, Patrick Daizel-Job, whose bold deeds while in combat combined a high degree of recklessness and bravery. The most notable departure from earlier spy fiction, which had focused on the gifted amateur acting on his own, lies in the hero's affiliation with a professional organization as a middle-grade civil servant. The deadly seriousness of the Cold War had imposed a much higher standard of set requirements than heretofore. Fleming also took pains to portray Bond as a modern, even classless hero, no longer part of the earlier clubland set but rather "a blunt instrument wielded by government department." Unlike his later cinematic embodiment, he was also prone to feelings of uncertainty and almost completely devoid of humor. "I never intended him to be a particularly likeable person," the author once wrote.[3]

After the publication of *Casino Royale*, 13 more Bond books appeared before the author's death of a heart attack in 1964. A quick writer who shunned introspection and self-criticism, he produced these novels on a regular annual basis, spending roughly two months in Jamaica during the late winter and keeping to a disciplined daily schedule. Clearly, readers relished the vivid fast-paced plots found in these pages, and the books ultimately sold more than 40 million copies, most of them during the latter part of his career. The American market received a major boost when a *Life Magazine* article revealed that President John F. Kennedy ranked *From Russia with Love* among his top ten all-time favorites. A subsequent advertisement showed a solitary light burning in the White House with the caption "You can bet on it he's reading one of those Ian Fleming thrillers."

Another keen admirer was Allen Dulles of the CIA who developed a friendship with the author – "a brilliant and witty talker, with ideas on everything."[4] Intrigued by some of the gadgetry, Dulles nevertheless gave Bond no chance of survival in a real-life confrontation with the Soviets. Whereas most literary critics judged the early novels quite favorably, a harsh backlash gradually took hold with complaints about excessive violence, vulgarity, snobbism, and a distinctly retrograde mindset. Still, the author had influential supporters on both sides of the Atlantic – among them Kingsley Amis (a later imitator), Noël Coward, Eric Ambler, and Raymond Chandler – accompanied by an expanding reading public.

Fleming once commented that he wrote "chiefly for pleasure, then for money."[5] But like many of his off-the-cuff remarks, considerably more lay beneath the surface. To his great consternation, he saw British influence rapidly receding in the postwar world and feared that the country was becoming no more than a soft and coddled spectator. In many respects, the Bond saga signified an effort to re-instill the indomitable fighting spirit of his fellow citizens that had prevailed during World War II and that had so decisively shaped his own outlook. In taking stock of the new Cold War realities, Fleming recognized that American ascendancy could be harnessed, not challenged, as seen in the basically cooperative relationship between Bond and his CIA counterpart Felix Leiter, who plays a recurring but conspicuously subordinate role.

Overt hostility to Soviet motives and methods figured most prominently in *From Russia with Love* – the only novel with a preface attesting to the semi-veracity of the plot. But from 1960 onward, SMERSH (Death to Spies) – the fearsome Soviet counterintelligence unit – was replaced by SPECTRE (Special Executive for Counterintelligence Terrorism, Revenge and Extortion) – an international crime syndicate operating independently of the East–West power bloc. For staunch anticommunists, this dramatic shift to imaginary, politically neutral opponents, however ruthless and megalomaniacal their schemes, proved a major disappointment. In a similar vein, the Soviet penetration of the Secret Intelligence Service, notably the revelations of the so-called Cambridge spies, found no prominent place. Only in *Casino Royale* did a double agent make an appearance, taking the form of Vesper Lynd, Bond's trusted personal assistant but in reality acting on behalf of SMERSH. Such reservations had little discernible impact, and it should not seem surprising that MI6 later enlisted Bond as a recruiting tool on its website.

The British writer generally considered the most potent antidote to Fleming is John le Carré. Born David Cornwell in Poole, he discovered at the age of 18 that his father was a high-living convicted embezzler responsible for a long string of bankruptcies. Since his mother had abandoned the family 15 years earlier, he and his brother found themselves turned into "fake gentry." "We arrived in educated middle-class society feeling almost like spies, knowing that we had no social hinterland, that we had a great deal to conceal and a lot of pretending to do."[6] After national service in the intelligence corps in Austria interrogating refugees fleeing from Hungary and Czechoslovakia, le Carré attended Oxford and obtained a first in modern languages in 1956. Two years teaching French and German at Eton were followed by his late entry into the Foreign Office, which provided cover for some light work as an intelligence operative.

Le Carré's subsequent posting in Germany – two and a half years in Bonn and one year in Hamburg – proved crucial for much of his writing, especially his breakthrough novel, *The Spy Who Came in from the Cold*, in 1963. In interviews, he stated that his *nom de plume* was simply taken from a London shop front he once passed on a bus, although he later contended that it came from nowhere in particular. The plot centers on Alec Leamas, a world-weary MI6 operative who, after helplessly witnessing the death of his top East German agent at a West Berlin border crossing, is summoned back to London – "in from the cold" – and given new instructions. According to Control, the unscrupulous SIS chief of service, Leamas is to let his personal life conspicuously degenerate and then fake a defection in order to save Hans-Dieter Mundt, the head of East German intelligence but also Britain's most prized double agent.

Even though the tautly constructed story takes a number of quite unexpected twists and turns, the reader can hardly fail to grasp the larger message. As Leamas bitterly explains to Liz Gold, his communist librarian girlfriend, "There's only one law in this game. ... Leninism – the expediency of temporary alliances. What do you think spies are: priests, saints, and martyrs? They're a squalid procession of vain fools, traitors too, yes; pansies, sadists and drunkards, people who play cowboys and Indians to brighten their rotten lives." The poignant conclusion at the eastern side of the Berlin Wall only serves to underscore the bleak tone that pervades the book.

Le Carré never concealed his contempt for the figure of James Bond – "the consumer-goods hero ... an unconscious but pretty accurate reflection of some of the worst things in western society."[7] Yet he also conceded that Fleming had stimulated an appetite in the public – one which his novels then sought to satisfy by providing the serious commentary on the Cold War that Bond's creator had presumably failed to provide. At root was le Carré's conviction that the spy world constituted the central battlefield of the Cold War. This struggle, moreover, juxtaposed the West, with its overriding emphasis on the individual and the right to dissent, against an opponent professing an allegiance to the vision of a greater collective. By having to fight an aggressor with its own weapons – he argued – the West stood in acute danger of losing its core values and hence its rationale as a society worth defending. He regarded his function, not to advance a personal philosophy, but to hold up a mirror to his contemporaries.

The immediate financial success of *The Spy* allowed le Carré to retire from the Foreign Office and pursue a full-time career as a writer. Of the numerous spy novels that followed, none achieved greater recognition than *Tinker Tailor Soldier Spy* published in 1974. In a direct line of descent from the earlier work, the author elevated George Smiley from a minor character into the key protagonist attempting to track down a Soviet mole in the "Circus," his term for SIS headquarters employed throughout his novels. The book has a distinctly topical quality, as le Carré sought to come to terms with the recent Philby Affair by creating a traitor, Bill Haydon, whose fictional career bears a strong resemblance to that of the actual Soviet double agent. Some have speculated that Sir Maurice Oldfield – the head of SIS during the mid-1970s – provided the basis for Smiley's character, but a more convincing case points to le Carré himself. He certainly expressed his fondness for Smiley – a quietly talented, methodical professional who tried to balance his humanity with the demands of his service. As he once observed, "Good intelligence work is gradual and rests on a kind of gentleness." Perhaps not surprisingly, Smiley emerged the victor in *Tinker Tailor* and reappeared in four subsequent books – *Smiley's People*, *The Looking Glass War*, *The Honorable Schoolboy*, and *The Secret Pilgrim*. "I think he stands where I stand; he feels that to pit yourself against any 'ism' is to strike a posture which is itself ideological, and therefore offensive in terms of practical decency."

Le Carré has attracted effusive admirers as well as harsh critics. Some in the former camp have praised his unparalleled knack for conveying the complex labyrinths of the secret service bureaucracy (he maintains that his literary style arose from drafting telegrams and dispatches while in the Foreign Office only to see them undergo revisions by colleagues at every level). Others have lauded the psychological subtlety and depth of his characterizations, placing him alongside literary masters ranging from Balzac to Solzhenitsyn. Those expressing serious misgivings have included leading intelligence professionals from both sides of the Iron Curtain. Kim Philby described the entire plot of *The Spy* as "basically implausible – at any rate to anyone who has any real knowledge of the business,"[8] while Richard Helms of the CIA took strong exception to the book's mood of despair and defeatism. The author further showed no appreciation in any of his works for the crucial role of technical collection. As several critics have cautioned, by no means should his pervasive cynicism be mistaken for realism. Le Carré admitted himself that his novels arose primarily from his imagination and did not necessarily correspond to actual people and situations. Nearly all of the espionage terms employed – "the lamplighters" and "the scalp-hunters," for example – were similarly his own coinage. "I invented a technical jargon that would be graphic and at the same time mysterious."[9]

Another author gaining international acclaim was Len Deighton, who created the intriguing figure of Bernard Samson, the son of a British army officer who organized a military security service in Berlin after 1945. Beginning with *Berlin Game* in 1982, Samson appeared in three trilogies spanning more than a decade. Having been raised and schooled in Berlin, he has never acquired an Oxbridge education, which puts him at odds with his colleagues at SIS (or "the Department," as Deighton phrased it) and limits his chances of promotion. Much of the drama revolves around the true allegiance of Samson's wife, Fiona, a fellow SIS operative who defects to East Germany in the first trilogy. A prodigious researcher, Deighton designed his novels on a large canvas involving a wide variety of characters. Meticulously depicted, the divided city itself plays a key role, and the issue of German unification is never very far from view. He also strove to minimize the descriptive passages and place primary emphasis on developing the dialogue – one filled with wit, sarcasm, and boundless treachery and deceit.

For the reader, plots within plots seemed to appear with each succeeding volume. In the sixth novel (*Spy Sinker*), for example, the narration shifts from Samson to the third person and recounts the events of the previous books, thereby calling into question the reliability of the version he had provided. Or in the final trilogy – *Faith*, *Hope*, and *Charity* – the same events are told from three different perspectives. Praise for Deighton's work has been voiced by both professional historians such as A. J. P. Taylor and fellow writers such as Julian Symons, who termed him as "a kind of poet of the spy story."[10]

Another shift in mood occurred in 1971 with the unexpected but rapid success of Frederick Forsyth's *The Day of the Jackal* – a novel that depicted the attempted assassination of Charles de Gaulle by a terrorist engaged by the Organisation Armée Secrete (Secret Armed Organization), an underground group angered by the country's abandonment of French Algeria. Applying the thorough research techniques learned as a foreign correspondent in Paris and East Berlin – and admitting his own lack of imagination to "spin a character out of the air" – he concentrated on weaving intricate plots arising from actual events. A work dealing directly with the East–West nuclear confrontation, *The*

Fourth Protocol (1984), proceeds from the premise – advanced in the book by Kim Philby, then a Moscow resident – that "the political stability of Great Britain is constantly overestimated," especially by the Soviet leadership. In a requested memorandum to the general secretary of the USSR, Philby outlines the Leninist techniques of subterfuge that could produce a revolutionary hard-left government in Britain and cause the collapse of the NATO alliance. As Plan Aurora evolves, Forsyth effectively describes the unmasking by SIS of a "false flag" recruitment[11] – in this case, a staunch anti-communist in the British Defense Ministry who believed that he was funneling crucial documents to a sympathetic South African diplomat, but in actuality, a KGB operative.

Although Germany provided the setting for countless Cold War spy novels, the number of German-language titles remained unusually sparse. One important exception was *Lieb Vaterland magst ruhig sein* (translated as *Dear Fatherland*) by the highly popular Austrian writer Georg Mario Simmel. Set in 1964, the story centers on the early tunneling efforts that enabled many East Germans to flee to the West. In addition to unsparing descriptions of political corruption on both sides of the wall, spies from various countries can be found among the large cast of characters. The main protagonist, however, is merely a small-time crook who unwittingly becomes involved in the East–West power struggle. And as it turns out, the tunnels actually form part of a major GDR operation designed to destabilize the Federal Republic by infiltrating a massive number of East German spies across the border.

From the other side of the Atlantic came another important variation of the spy novel with the appearance of *The Hunt for Red October* by Tom Clancy in 1984. The term "techno-thriller" is often used to describe his works, even though Clancy himself considered it a misnomer. Nevertheless, the plots – simultaneously simple yet complex – are laced with detailed scientific and technical descriptions, leading many readers to suspect that he had privileged access to classified defense data. But Clancy, by background an independent insurance agent in Maryland, always maintained that his information derived primarily from open-source trade publications such as the *Aerospace Daily* or *Jane's Intelligence Weekly*. Couched generally in lay language, these descriptions, however, never overpowered the story line, which, by means of succinct, rapidly changing scenes from multiple perspectives, maintained a high level of suspense. In addition, Clancy demonstrated the ability to make some implausible situations sound quite credible. "I've made up stuff that's turned out to be real, that's the spooky part."[12]

Inspired by a recent incident, *The Hunt for Red October* marked the beginning of the saga of Jack Ryan – a CIA data analyst and former marine, stockbroker, and history professor. In this instance, he assisted with the defection of Marko Ramius, a half-Lithuanian naval captain and commander of the most advanced ballistic missile submarine in the Soviet fleet – specifically a *Typhoon*-class vessel equipped with a revolutionary stealth propulsion system almost undetectable by existing sonar systems. A major challenge facing the Americans was how to contact and acquire this "silent predator" without killing those crew members wishing to return to the USSR and without Soviet officials in Moscow discovering what was afoot. In the novels that followed – Jack Ryan reappeared in nine of them and eventually became president of the United States – Clancy never suppressed his fundamental enmity toward the Soviet system, but he also issued some sharp criticisms of Western intelligence agencies. His initial success was aided by President Ronald Reagan, who described *The Hunt for Red October* as "a perfect yarn." It is noteworthy, too, that Clancy dedicated his 1996 novel, *Executive Orders*, to Reagan, calling him "the man who won the war."

The closest counterpart to Ian Fleming in the Eastern bloc – particularly in terms of popularity – was Julian Semyonov (Lyandres), born in Moscow in 1931. Despite a degree from the Oriental Institute of Moscow University, his much preferred vocation was fiction writing. Semyonov's earliest works dealt mostly with crime and the work of Russian police investigators, leading to his first major success, *Petrovka 38*, the address of the central Moscow police station. Yet, the vast readership that soon developed remember him best for espionage novels such as *Tass Is Authorized to Announce. ...* , which, published in 1979, revolves around the CIA's attempt – in collusion with a multinational firm – to stage a coup in the allegorical African country of Nagonia and oust its black Marxist leader.

Earlier, however, with active encouragement from the KGB chairman at the time, Yuri Andropov, Semyonov had embarked on his famed multi-volume Stirlitz series. Born in Switzerland of exiled Russian parents and personally recruited by Feliks Dzerzhinsky, the founder of the Cheka, Maxim Stirlitz assumes a number of aliases in the course of his perilous spy career. Without doubt he strikingly embodies the most desirable attributes of the Soviet spy: sensitive, courageous, deeply patriotic, physically adroit, well educated, and, above all, perspicacious. He always keeps the key objective uppermost in his mind, knowing that the collapse of a single link in an overly predetermined plan could doom the whole mission. Also, in contrast to the author, who was strongly drawn to the personal machismo of Ernest Hemingway, Stirlitz remains faithfully married to his wife, even when the couple are separated after the birth of their son. He is a composite character, according to Semyonov, and cannot be traced to a single individual.

The two most popular books in the series – *Seventeen Moments of Spring* and its sequel *The Order Is to Survive* – take place in Berlin and Switzerland during the final months of the war. Assuming the identity of an SS officer named Max Otto von Stirlitz, he gains an important position in the foreign intelligence division, which allows him to witness the secret negotiations between leading Nazis and the Western allies and to keep the "Center" in Moscow fully informed. Construed as an outright betrayal of the alliance with the Soviet Union, the action centers on the meetings between Karl Wolff, the chief SS commander in Italy, and Allen Dulles, the American OSS chief of station in Bern. All the while, Stirlitz must navigate among quarreling factions in the Reich Security Office and diffuse the mounting suspicions of his superiors, Ernst Kaltenbrunner and Heinrich Müller, regarding his true identity.

The narrative style of Semyonov's novels, which he termed "political chronicles," relies on the copious insertion of historical information, sometimes taking the form of entire documents. For the Russian public, this approach held an unusual fascination. The number of Soviet historical works on Nazi Germany – whether dealing with Hitler, the Gestapo, the party elite, or life in general – was almost nonexistent, and Semyonov's books handily filled that void. With the fictional field virtually his alone, he moved beyond the standard Soviet caricatures of Nazi officials and other foreign figures and constructed psychologically credible characters, some not lacking in redeeming characteristics. At one point, for example, Stirlitz contradicts a colleague's assertion that all Germans are Hitlerites. "If I shared your opinion I would immediately ask the 'Center' for a transfer to another assignment. There are good Germans just as there are people of great integrity and high moral standards among the Russian émigrés."

At the same time, a knowledgeable reader will detect numerous factual errors that crop up along the way. As one commentator noted, Stirlitz would not have traveled in a non-occupied country like Yugoslavia in his black SS uniform, nor was there a Soviet embassy in Switzerland in 1945, nor did Allen Dulles head the CIA the following year.[13] In addition, some of the plot lines reveal a more sinister interpretation of events than was actually the case, and not a few of the purported documents were a product of the author's fertile imagination.

Nonetheless, Semyonov's achievement is most remarkable. He became more widely read than most other writers of his era – a total of 35 million copies of 60 books or so was published – and received the USSR's highest literary award. While certain ideological boundaries could not be crossed – such as mentioning Stalin's contemptuous dismissal of repeated warnings of Hitler's attack in June 1941 – Semyonov occasionally ventured beyond what was officially sanctioned. Probably most remarkable of all, his creation of Stirlitz has become an integral part of contemporary Russian folklore, surviving all the vicissitudes of the country's history since the author's death in 1990. Debuting on Soviet television in 1973, the 12-part serialization of *Seventeen Moments of Spring* elicited an overwhelming response from viewers and only added to the cult status of the main character.

Contrary to the development of the modern spy novel, the first films made their appearance in the United States during World War I. Even though war with Germany had not yet been declared, the threat posed by enemy agents was vividly depicted in *Our Secret Wires* (1915), *The Hero of Submarine D-2* (1916), *As In a Looking Glass* (1916), and *The Secret of the Submarine* (1916). American involvement in the war then sparked films such as *The Greatest Power* (1917) in which Ethel Barrymore discovered her lover to be a German spy – part of a wideranging plot to establish secret submarine bases off the New England coast and to sabotage war-related factories through German-born aliens. And it was in Weimar Germany in 1928 that the most notable spy film of the silent era appeared – Fritz Lang's epic *Spione* (*Spies*). Inspired by the subversive activities of a Soviet trade delegation at the time, Lang placed at the center of the labyrinthine plot the arch-villain Haghi, an outwardly respectable bank director who in reality headed a vast espionage network. Then with the release of the first of numerous anti-Nazi spy films – *Confessions of a Nazi Spy* (1939) – Hollywood introduced the technique of injecting actual newsreel footage into the dramatized story.

But it was nevertheless the British who made the most enduring contributions to the genre, especially during the Cold War period. Foremost among all directors was Alfred Hitchcock, who, prior to his arrival in Hollywood in 1939, had already directed five well-received spy melodramas. "My hero," he once stated, "is the average man to whom bizarre things happen, rather than vice versa."[14] He further noted his indebtedness to Edgar Allan Poe as well as screenwriters possessing a background in British military intelligence. And he once likened his own "sinister" motives as a director to that of a spy who had "wormed my way into my pictures ... I manage that by shifting to the front side of the camera and letting my company shoot me, so I can see what it is like to be shot by my company."[15]

In the immediate postwar period, Hitchcock continued an anti-fascist theme in *Notorious* – a brooding romantic thriller that struck a strong chord with the public. Here, according to the director, the film focuses on "a woman caught in a web of world events from which she could not extricate herself."[16] The struggle pits the US government against a group of Nazi spies in Buenos Aires attempting to build a nuclear bomb, even though at times the heroine seems to be the tragic pawn of both groups. An ambitious remake of the earlier *The 39 Steps* was entitled *The Man Who Knew Too Much* (1956) – this time partially shot on location in North Africa, featuring an American couple at the center of the plot and dramatizing a close collaborative effort between British and French intelligence. A classic thriller-comedy, *North by Northwest* (1959), hinged on a CIA scheme to infiltrate a Soviet espionage ring and cast the main protagonist as the victim of mistaken identity, forced to flee from both the spies and the police. Particularly memorable are two chase scenes orchestrated by the spymasters, one involving a crop-dusting airplane, the other taking place on the precipices of Mount Rushmore.

Two later Hitchcock films dealt with the realities of the Cold War in more explicit terms, even though they fall below what is generally considered his finest work. One is *Torn Curtain* (1966), which, unlike his other espionage films, utilizes an original screenplay written under his careful supervision. It depicts the mission of Michael Armstrong, an American nuclear scientist turned spy and dispatched to East Germany. By feigning his disillusionment with Washington's "belligerent" policies and defecting to the communist side, he gains a position with an acclaimed researcher at the University of Leipzig, who is developing a defensive weapon that will render all offensive nuclear weapons obsolete. One of the most striking episodes reveals the prolonged difficulty that Armstrong and his female accomplice face in disposing of a determined antagonist. In this regard, Hitchcock specifically wanted to distance himself from the James Bond films, which, in his view, made the killing of human beings all too simple and routine. Also prominent is the director's anti-communist outlook. East Germany possesses all the trappings of an omnipotent police state, as further underscored by the existence of "Pi," an underground pro-Western resistance network supporting Armstrong's mission.

The other film is *Topaz* (1969), based on the best-selling novel by Leon Uris. Set at the time of the Cuban Missile Crisis, the plot intertwines a number of actual events and transforms a former French intelligence officer, Philippe Thyraud de Vosjoli, into the central character, André Deveraux, who is willing to ignore his superiors and cooperate with the CIA. Two main themes dominate: the confirmation of the Soviet missile installation in October 1962, and the revelation of enemy penetration of the Western democracies. The title, in fact, derives from the spy ring "Sapphire" (alias Topaz) that had infiltrated the upper echelons of the French government. Another important spy in the film was inspired by the Soviet defector Anatoliy Golitsyn. In presenting him as the character Boris Kusenov, Hitchcock showed the man's arrogant and demanding personality but then chose to omit the increasingly far-fetched conspiracy theories that Golitsyn confided to the CIA and the considerable turmoil that resulted. Rather, the director's primary objective was to reassure the viewer of American competence through the successful resolution of both crises.

A final item bears mentioning, even though the film was canceled in 1979, never having gone beyond the preproduction stage owing to Hitchcock's failing health. Utilizing a novel of the same name along with a nonfiction study, *The Short Night* focuses on the spectacular escape from London's Wormwood Scrubs Prison by George Blake, the British SIS officer given a 42-year sentence for spying for the KGB ("a year for each life betrayed" in the court's verdict, although some authorities place the number much higher). In the planned film, the Blake figure, Gavin Brand, flees to Finland to reunite with his wife and two young sons. Yet, Joe Bailey, the older brother of a CIA operative who became one of Brand's victims, has been reluctantly recruited by the Americans to pursue the fugitive – an adventure that entails a torrid affair with Brand's wife, her attempted murder by a hitman engaged by the Soviets, and a fevered concluding chase toward the Finnish–Russian border. Hitchcock's utter lack of sympathy for the fictional Brand stands in sharp contrast to the British film director, Tony Richardson, who, according to those found responsible for Blake's escape, had provided them with all the necessary funds, not the KGB.[17]

A spy film that gained legendary status within the Eastern bloc was *For Eyes Only – streng geheim* (top secret). Produced in 1963 by DEFA – the East German state film studio – it featured a double agent named Hansen who, posing as a defector, managed to gain a posting at the US Military Intelligence (here MID) unit in Würzburg, itself disguised as a commercial trading firm. The film's concept can be traced to the earlier case of Horst Hesse, who succeeded in bringing a large cache of confidential US military documents back to the GDR and later writing his memoirs. Although party functionaries prevented the screenplay's author from consulting with Hesse, the opening credits ironically allude to the case: "The action in this film is completely fictitious – any resemblance to actual events and living people is intentional."

Hansen's assignment was to obtain an original copy of the purported plans of the US Army to launch a massive military offensive against the GDR. Even though he came under suspicion by his American superiors – and must surmount a complete blockade of the routes leading back to East Berlin – Hansen's mission was ultimately successful. Noteworthy, too, is the bitter rivalry emphasized in the film between the Americans and the West German BND (purported to be composed solely of unreconstructed Nazis). By then passing on this document to the international press corps, the East Germans thus thwarted the American plan in its infancy. While no known evidence confirms the existence of such a contingency – Hesse's documents had led only to the unmasking of 137 Western agents in the GDR – the film provided ample propagandistic justification for the recent construction of the Berlin Wall. During the next ten years, *For Eyes Only* attracted 2.3 million viewers alone in the GDR. While the Stasi desired the production of more feature films of this nature – those that posed a stark black-and-white contrast with the Western services, even in the décor, costumes, and music – none came close to matching the caliber of this work.

The most auspicious moment in the development of postwar spy films occurred with the arrival of James Bond in British movie theaters in 1962. The first three entries – *Dr. No, From Russia with Love*, and *Goldfinger* – were released in consecutive years to enthusiastic audiences, sharply reversing a downward trend in British cinema attendance (Americans were somewhat slower in their initial response). Generally regarded as the best of the entire series, they bear the closest resemblance to Fleming's novels and established the basic formula that was to be followed in subsequent efforts – tongue-in-cheek dialogue, exotic foreign locales, ingenious gadgetry, formidable villains, and a sizable quantity of sex and violence. Terrence Young, the director of the first two films, however, described how he began the project with no clear conception in mind. "The only way I thought we could do a Bond film was to heat it up, give it a sense of humour, to make it as cynical as possible."[18] Both he and his producer were convinced, in any event, that the mundane social realism of the so-called "kitchen sink dramas" had run its course and a new type of film was needed.

Over time, just as the actors selected to portray Bond changed on a regular basis, so, too, there were noticeable adjustments to the generic formula, usually mirroring prevailing social and political attitudes. One can discern, for example, how the plots at times followed the ebb and flow of East–West tensions. The 1977 film, *The Spy Who Loved Me*, embraced the then-current policy of détente and showed Bond working in league with Agent Triple X of the KGB – Major Anya Amasova – to investigate the disappearance of their country's submarines and ultimately avert the nuclear holocaust being plotted by the proto-Nazi megalomaniac Karl Stromberg. The next film, *For Your Eyes Only*, appeared in 1981, as superpower relations had entered a far more bellicose phase. In this instance, Bond's antagonist is a Soviet-backed villain attempting to obtain an ultra-low-frequency coded transmitting device – a so-called Automatic Targeting Attack Communicator – from a British spy ship accidentally sunk off the coast of Albania. The cast also includes an East German biathlon champion – Erich Kriegler – as a determined KGB assassin. In the climax, after Bond destroys the device by tossing it off a steep precipice in Greece, he remarks to KGB head, General Anatol Gogol, "That's détente, comrade. You don't have it – I don't have it."

Above all, the Bond series must be reckoned as the most successful cinematic franchise in history, maintaining a consistent record over a long span of time with seemingly no end in sight. Various estimates have established that between one quarter and one half of the world's population have viewed a Bond film, either in a movie theater, on television, or via a DVD.[19] The Bond phenomenon may well be the most persuasive explanation of why so many regard the British to be preeminent in the field of espionage.

A prize-winning German film that made a deep impression in the post-unification period was *Das Leben der Anderen* (*The Lives of Others*) written and directed by Florian Henckel von Donnersmarck. Set in East Berlin during the mid- to late-1980s, it depicts the methodical Stasi surveillance of a playwright suspected of disloyalty to the regime and his actress girlfriend. The pivotal character turns out to be Captain Gerd Wiesler, the case officer assigned to monitor them from a listening post in the apartment building's attic. In the course of his eavesdropping, he undergoes a personal conversion – sparked by the music and poetry he overhears – and attempts to aid the targeted couple. Critics correctly pointed out that, among other discrepancies, there was no known case of a Stasi officer acting in the manner suggested by the film. The director, however, defended his dramatic license, maintaining that art should not be a literal representation of reality but needs to be concentrated or thickened (*verdichtet*) at certain points. It also should indicate how one could behave if such a situation ever arose. Not to have given Wiesler the possibility of a free choice would have rendered him a victim of the system – a defense that many Stasi officers advanced after the Stasi was dissolved.

The spy genre readily found a home on American television, never achieving, however, the same degree of prominence as such staples as westerns, detective and police series, and medical dramas. Of the espionage shows debuting in the 1950s, *I Led Three Lives* quickly gained the dominant position and attracted a wide audience. Based upon an autobiography of the same name, it depicted the life of Herbert A. Philbrick, a Boston advertising executive who, for nine years, had infiltrated the US Communist Party as an FBI informant. Richard Carlson, in the role of Philbrick, narrated each of the 117 syndicated episodes, using a clipped voice-over to impart a semi-documentary tone as well as to heighten the suspense. A typical half-hour show might feature communist plans to introduce a low-cost narcotic to American youngsters, to procure a new atomic device from a defense plant, or to incite labor unrest by distributing incendiary pamphlets among factory workers.

From all accounts, J. Edgar Hoover regarded the series quite highly, although, contrary to rumors, it was never vetted by the FBI, and he publicly disavowed any official connection. Philbrick himself reviewed the plot outlines and provided other technical assistance. When asked to testify before Joseph McCarthy's Senate committee at the time, he declined, stating that the Wisconsin politician "had harmed the cause of anti-Communism more than anyone I know."[20] Early on, the series drew a sharp distinction between liberalism and communism, which Philbrick believed would extend the program's appeal to leading anti-communist intellectuals. "If the inexperienced Red hunter cannot distinguish between a Communist and an innocent liberal," he stated, "then he is also unable to distinguish a bona-fide Communist from a government counterspy ... it takes experts to fight experts."[21]

One oddity of this period was an episode from the live anthology drama series *Climax!*. Viewers received their first glimpse of James Bond in a screen adaptation of Fleming's *Casino Royale*. Albeit condensed, the basic plot remained intact with the exception of the Americanization of Bond and the Anglicization of Clarence Leiter, now affiliated with the SIS instead of the CIA. This reversal seems understandable, given the fact that it was an American production for an American audience and the Bond cultural phenomenon had hardly begun. What critics most prized was the casting of the well-known character actor Peter Lorre as the Soviet operative, Le Chiffre. In addition, some even feel that the somber tone and spare sets better captured the mood and suspense of the original novel than the later films. Afterwards, Fleming, having written treatments for 13 episodes, tried to negotiate a regular series on American television, but the project never came to fruition.

When Bond made his eventual transition to the cinema, the impact upon American television was immediate. The mid-1960s came to represent the high-water mark for spy-related programs. In one instance, the title character of the popular series *Burke's Law*, who operated as a California detective for the first two seasons, suddenly became a globetrotting employee of a US government intelligence agency. But it was a new program – veering away from the stark superpower confrontation of the Cold War – that attracted an even larger viewership. In *The Man from U.N.C.L.E.*, the complex organization striving to maintain political and legal order throughout the world enlisted its members without regard to national background (one of the three main characters, Nickovitch Kuryakin, was originally conceived as a Soviet agent). U.N.C.L.E.'s most frequent opponent was THRUSH, an international power with no allegiance to a particular country or political philosophy but possessing a vast army of pawns and bent on acquiring the latest technological weaponry.

Another long-running American series attaining wide audience appeal was *Mission: Impossible*, which chronicled the covert assignments of a small team of secret agents – the Impossible Missions Force – overseen by an undisclosed government or organization. The episodes made no explicit reference to any country in the Soviet bloc but employed fictitious names such as the "European People's Republic" and "Eastern European Republic" to designate enemy states. Briskly paced, the series shunned character development from the outset and purposely kept humor out of the scripts in order to concentrate more fully on the exploit at hand. Sophisticated, technically plausible gadgetry – usually derived from professional journals – also had a conspicuous part.

The most successful of all the televised spy shows was *The Avengers*, a thoroughly British production in terms of its concept, casting, setting, and innovative visual style. At the height of its popularity in the late 1960s, it was seen by an estimated 30 million viewers in 70 different countries. With his trademark steel-lined bowler hat and sword-in-the-handle umbrella, John Steed, the central male character, although independently wealthy, engaged in undercover work as a professional activity, not as a gentlemanly diversion, while three of his partners – Cathy Gale, Emma Peel, and Tara King – became celebrated for their intelligence and technical skills, as well as their charming and graceful manner. A young widow with a doctorate in anthropology and a black belt in judo, Gale evoked particular praise from feminist commentators, who hailed her coequal status as a milestone in television casting. In terms of content, *The Avengers* preferred to play on the tensions of the Cold War without exploring its ideological substance. And as the series evolved, narrative conventions were overturned in order to confound the audience's expectations. The psychological realism of the early years gave way to increasingly bizarre storylines and eccentric characterizations.

For many serious viewers, the most authentic series ever to appear on television was *The Sandbaggers* – 20 fast-moving episodes produced by Yorkshire Television and broadcast in the United Kingdom during the period of 1978–1980 (they later appeared in the United States via public television). While the title referred to highly trained covert operatives dispatched throughout the world on dangerous assignments, most of the complex drama took place in the offices of the Secret Intelligence Service in London and arose from political struggles, double crosses, and personality clashes. As Neil Burnside, the central character and an ex-Sandbagger himself, once remarked: "Our battles aren't fought at the end of a parachute. They're won and lost in the drab, dreary corridors in Westminster. ... If you want James Bond, go to your library, but if you want a successful operation, sit at your desk and think, and then think again." In this austere setting, Burnside had no modern computerized equipment at his disposal. Demanding, intelligent, and ambitious, he was very protective of his men in the field, always exercising caution and discretion before sending them on a mission, but also not hesitant to circumvent his superiors whenever deemed necessary.

Production abruptly stopped in July 1979 after the unclarified disappearance of Ian Mackintosh, the originator and principal screenwriter of the series. A former Royal Navy lieutenant commander with a background in intelligence, he disappeared mysteriously along with two companions while on board a small plane over the Gulf of Alaska. Even though the series had a relatively short run, MacKintosh had created a sharply defined protagonist along with an avid following. The earnest tone of his scripts conveyed a documentary-like impression and mirrored several of the author's strongly held convictions. Not uncritical of the Western services, he nevertheless saw the Soviet Union as the chief adversary. Because of its complete lack of scruples, Burnside never thought in terms of fair play and had no qualms in trying to sabotage the Strategic Arms Limitation Talks in the final episode of the series. The high value that Mackintosh accorded the "special relationship" between the United States and Great Britain was underscored as well. As he noted in his original outline, "The SIS's only real partner is the CIA ... and the SIS could not function properly without it."[22] In arguably the most controversial episode, Burnside was even willing to sacrifice the sole female Sandbagger (with whom he had fallen in love) in order to preserve it.

Predictions that the end of the Cold War would deliver a fatal blow to the genre of spy fiction and film quickly turned out to be wide of the mark. The bestseller lists of the 1990s still featured established writers such as le Carré and Forsyth, while newcomers such as Alan Furst and Daniel Silva received much critical acclaim. As Somerset Maugham stated in the original preface to *Ashenden*, "But there will always be espionage and there will always be counter-espionage." Nonetheless, it seems undeniable that the Cold War provided a uniquely suited historical backdrop that will not be easily replicated in the future.

Notes

1 Cited by Ben Macintyre, *For Your Eyes Only: Ian Fleming and James Bond* (London: Bloomsbury Publishing, 2008), 107.
2 Cited by Macintyre, *For Your Eyes Only*, 104.
3 Cited by Macintyre, *For Your Eyes Only*, 204.
4 Allen Dulles, *Great Spy Stories* (Secaucus, NJ: Castle, 1969), 361.
5 "How to Write a Thriller" in *Books and Bookmen*, May, 1963.
6 Matthew J. Bruccoli and Judith S. Baughman (Eds), *Conversations with John le Carré* (Jackson, MS: University Press of Mississippi, 2004), 65.
7 *Conversations*, 7.
8 Cited by Hugh Trevor-Roper, *The Philby Affair: Espionage, Treason, and Secret Services* (London: Kimber, 1968), 61.
9 *Conversations*, 69.
10 Cited by David Stafford, *The Silent Game: The Real World of Imaginary Spies* (Athens, GA: University of Georgia Press, 1988), 225.
11 "False flag" refers to a deliberate misrepresentation by a recruiter to gain a more favorable reception by a potential agent.
12 *New York Times*, July 27, 1986.
13 Walter Laqueur, *Soviet Realties: Culture and Politics from Stalin to Gorbachev* (New Brunswick, NJ: Transaction Publishers, 1990), 219–220.
14 Cited by Gene D. Phillips, *Alfred Hitchcock* (Boston, MA: Twayne Publishers, 1984), 20.
15 *Hitchcock on Hitchcock: Selected Writings and Interviews* (Berkeley, CA: University of California Press, 1995), 122.
16 *Hitchcock on Hitchcock*, 104.
17 Nigel West, *At Her Majesty's Secret Service: The Chiefs of Britain's Intelligence Agency MI6* (Annapolis, MD: Naval Institute Press, 2006), 104.
18 Cited by James Chapman, *Licence to Thrill: A Cultural History of the James Bond Films* (London: I. B. Tauris, 2007), 56.
19 Cited by Chapman, *Licence to Thrill*, 13.
20 *Boston Globe*, August 18, 1993.
21 Cited by Thomas Patrick Doherty, *Cold War, Cool Medium, McCarthyism, and American Culture* (New York, NY: Columbia University Press, 2003), 141.
22 Cited by Robert G. Folsom, *The Life and Mysterious Death of Ian Mackintosh: The Inside Story of the Sandbaggers and Television's Top Spy* (Dulles, VA: Potomac Books, 2012), 29.

7 The Climax of the Cold War

In retrospect, it was the election of Karol Wojtyla, the former Cardinal-Archbishop of Kracków, as Pope John Paul II in October 1978 that portended the end of the communist regime in Poland – the largest of the satellite states – and initiated the disintegration of the remainder of the Soviet bloc. Alarm bells immediately sounded at KGB headquarters, for the ranking Catholic cleric had for years been under close surveillance by the Polish SB and was nearly prosecuted for making seditious statements during his sermons. The SB reports had further noted the force of his personality, the keenness of his intellect, and the intensity of his spirituality. Upon hearing the news of his election to the Holy See, KGB chief Andropov issued a somber warning; "Wojtyla represents a menace to Soviet security."[1] Andropov's fears soon began to find realization, notably when John Paul returned to Poland during the first year of his pontificate and attracted more than 10 million people – one third of the country's entire population – during his nine-day visit. Increasingly, the conviction grew among Soviet officials that as long as a Polish pope existed, communism would never take root in the country.

To counter this new papal threat, the KGB received instructions from the Politburo to organize propaganda campaigns in the Eastern bloc emphasizing how Vatican policies were undermining traditional Catholic doctrines and practices. Through its own agents in the Vatican, the SB sought to sow internal discord and to persuade the pope to support international détente as defined by Moscow. But to the consternation of both the KGB and the SB, a new source of dissent appeared with the rise of Solidarity (*Solidarnosc*) – an independent, self-governing trade union that began to function in the Gdansk shipyard in June 1980 under the leadership of a 37-year-old electrician, Lech Wałesa. Moreover – with the quiet but unmistakable endorsement of the Pope – Solidarity achieved formal recognition by the Polish government two months later with the signing of the Gdansk Accords. For the KGB and the Politburo, such an unprecedented event signified "the legalization of the anti-Socialist opposition" and posed the most acute threat since the Prague Spring of 1968.

The gravity of the situation was also not lost on Poland's immediate neighbor to the west, East Germany, whose intelligence service had been scrupulously monitoring the rising level of dissent in the country during the 1970s. The head of the HVA, Markus Wolf, could boast of sources of information in Wałesa's circle and that of the leading intellectual Adam Michnik. In addition to the expulsion of all Polish guest workers from the GDR, these new developments prompted the creation of special working groups inside the ministry headquarters and in the provincial offices along the now closed Polish border. Their main objective was to assess the support that Solidarity was receiving from outside the country. Two outlets were deemed most subversive: the Polish service of Radio Free Europe, the country's largest source of uncensored information whose broadcasts reached nearly half of the adult population; and *Kultura*, which was edited by a small group of émigrés in a Paris suburb. It counted as the most influential and widely read Polish-language journal and provided a forum to debate oppositional strategy and tactics. By 1980 the HVA had launched its own counter-attack, which came to include fallacious copies of underground publications, defamatory rumors about Solidarity leaders, and forged letters insinuating that the exiled activists were leading an overly luxurious lifestyle in the West.

While visiting Rome in mid-May 1981, a young Turk named Memet Ali Agca fired a shot from a distance of 20 feet and nearly killed John Paul in St. Peter's Square. Had the bullet passed several millimeters closer to the central aorta, death would have been instantaneous. The would-be assassin appeared to have ties with Bulgarian intelligence, but the larger question of a further Soviet connection has yet to be answered conclusively. The new American DCI William Casey was firmly convinced of KGB involvement, which was advanced as well in the official report of the Italian state prosecutor's office. "In some secret place, where every secret is wrapped in another secret, some political figure of great power … mindful of the needs of the Eastern bloc, decided that it was necessary to kill Pope Wojtyla."[2]

Nevertheless, Casey's assistant and future DCI, Robert Gates – after conducting an exhaustive inquiry with the presumption of Soviet guilt – failed to uncover any hard evidence. The CIA's analytical report published in May 1985 left the question open – "one of the great remaining secrets of the Cold War" in Gates's words.[3] Among former KGB officials, opinion has been distinctly divided, some maintaining such a foolhardy endeavor would never have been seriously contemplated, others considering it well within the realm of probability. For its part, the democratic successor government of Bulgaria reviewed 124 volumes of surviving secret documents during the 1990s and found no convincing piece of evidence regarding its country's complicity.

Moscow continued to chafe at the seeming inaction of the Polish government vis-à-vis the growing strength of Solidarity – underscored in January 1981 by Wałesa's first of numerous private audiences with the Pope. Andropov was even receiving reports of related unrest occurring within the borders of the USSR. Finally, in mid-December – following more than a year of unrelenting pressure from the Soviets, not excluding the threat of military intervention – General Wojciech Jaruzelski, the former defense minister, assumed power as head of the Military Council for National Salvation and proclaimed martial law. It was the solution most favored by Moscow. Totally unprepared for anything as far-reaching as Operation X, top Solidarity leaders were suddenly arrested along with thousands of others. All telephone and telex communications were cut, key industries were placed under military control, and a dusk-to-dawn curfew was imposed in every major town. Jaruzelski credited the main success of the operation to the SB, which had deeply penetrated the opposition and provided the intelligence necessary "to neutralize the adversary by the swiftest means possible." The SB's main target remained Wałesa, who, through a series of fabrications, was portrayed as an avaricious, foul-mouthed embezzler.

With its makeshift but vital printing presses confiscated and radio stations closed, Solidarity had no alternative but to go underground and start from scratch. Initially the new Reagan administration, like its predecessor, viewed the unfolding events in Poland with much caution, fearful of injuring Solidarity's cause by a full-fledged show of support. That policy, however, changed significantly following the declaration of martial law. In September 1982, the administration charged the CIA with providing covert aid to Solidarity, reasoning that a banned organization that had earlier operated legally possessed a substantial psychological advantage over a dissident movement never having emerged from the shadows. Once the Jaruzelski regime lifted martial lawn in July 1983, a supplemental US program of overt aid was instituted through the National Endowment for Democracy, which relied on intermediaries such as the labor confederation AFL–CIO and the Polish-American Congress.

An element of secrecy still surrounds the details of the covert aid program, despite its incontrovertible success. No former Solidarity activist has volunteered information on what occurred, nor has the program received full acknowledgment by the CIA. According to Robert Gates's quasi-official confirmation in his memoirs, this aid took two forms: a global propaganda campaign to increase awareness of Solidarity's struggle; and a large supply of sophisticated printing and broadcasting equipment, indispensable in facilitating illicit domestic communications and keeping the movement alive. The larger objective – the so-called "long march" approach – aimed at the creation of an alternative underground society that avoided any direct confrontation with communist authorities (one important pamphlet by Czerslaw Bieecki writing under a pseudonym conveyed instructions on how to organize conspiratorial activities and how to behave if arrested and interrogated). Arguably the most ingenious piece of spyware developed by the CIA was a localized television transmitter capable of overriding the state-run network for several minutes. Employed during peak viewing periods (such as half-time in soccer matches), this device obscured the regular screen and allowed the Solidarity logo to appear accompanied by a spirited message. Viewers were then encouraged to switch their houselights on and off in quick succession as a signal of support.

The CIA established so-called "ratlines" (or clandestine channels) for conveying money and equipment into Poland. The Polish officer charged with monitoring Western intelligence services later maintained that the SB knew about most of this illicit traffic but refrained from making arrests in order to document the entire network and the recipients of the contraband. According to a commission appointed by the post-communist Polish parliament, none of the money and only about 30 percent of the equipment had been intercepted by the security forces, even though the underground had been partially penetrated. This appraisal seems all the more significant given the long duration of the secret aid from 1982 to 1988. KGB disinformation efforts to expose American interference in Polish affairs – such as Operation SIRENA 2 – had little if any impact, nor did similar attempts directed at Wałesa by the SB purporting to reveal his corruption and greed.

As the Cold War intensified on several fronts, the KGB leadership became firmly convinced that the United States was taking preparatory steps for launching a surprise nuclear attack. At a major conference in Moscow in May 1981, Andropov announced an unprecedented move – a new top-priority foreign intelligence operation in conjunction with the GRU. Codenamed RYAN (an acronym in Russian for Nuclear Rocket Attack), it was to collect all military-strategic data confirming the immediate nuclear threat posed by the United States and its NATO allies. A checklist of activities construed as suspicious – largely replicating the Soviet Union's own contingency plans for war with the West – was distributed to the residencies in NATO countries. Admittedly, some of the KGB's leading American experts – including the British defector Donald Maclean who composed a highly classified memorandum – regarded Andropov's fears as unduly alarmist, but their doubts fell on deaf ears. When Andropov replaced Brezhnev as the new Soviet leader the following year, his view of the US intentions hardened even more, particularly regarding Reagan, whom he considered an extreme and unpredictable adventurist.

In the early morning of September 1, 1983, the pilot of a South Korean Boeing 747 – flight KAL-007– unknowingly flew off course and drifted over forbidden Soviet territory while en route from New York to Seoul. Fearing that the intruder might have been a US reconnaissance plane, the Soviet air defense command ordered the pilot of an interceptor aircraft to fire a heat-seeking R-98 missile when perfunctory warnings went unnoticed by the Korean pilot. All 269 passengers and crew were killed as a result. The destruction of a civilian aircraft was a serious enough matter, but Moscow's twisting explanations only served to compound the problem, not least for the USSR's image abroad. Unwilling to acknowledge simply that an unfortunate accident had occurred – as urged by many in the foreign ministry – the chief of staff of the Soviet armed forces, Marshal Nikolai Ogarkov, stated unequivocally at a live televised press conference that the illegal intrusion was "a deliberate, carefully planned intelligence operation."[4]

The United States rejected this unfounded conspiracy theory out of hand. To make his case that the destruction of the aircraft was "an act of barbarism" by a society with scant regard for human rights and human life, Reagan gave a televised speech to the nation on September 5, playing excerpts of the intercepted radio communications of the pilot immediately before and after firing the missile. Never before had SIGINT been cited explicitly in a public presidential address. The following day, Jeane Kirkpatrick, the US ambassador to the United Nations, utilized even lengthier excerpts in an audio-visual presentation to the General Assembly. Dismissing such evidence as "imperialist propaganda," Andropov doggedly persisted with the accusation that the United States was guilty of an "insidious provocation involving a South Korean plane engineered by US special services."

This rapidly escalating tension between the United States and the Soviet Union culminated in a perilous episode that, unlike the earlier Cuban Missile Crisis, escaped public notice. NATO routinely held full military exercises that were carefully monitored by Soviet intelligence – particularly since Moscow's own contingency plans for a surprise attack against the West regarded such exercises as camouflage for an actual strike. The NATO exercises that took place in early November 1983 – designated

Able Archer – differed noticeably from previous ones. Even though no troop or nuclear weapons movements were involved, an altered message format – combined with radio silence at several bases – indicated to alarmed Soviet analysts that American forces had been placed on alert. Fearing that the countdown to a nuclear war had already commenced, the KGB and the GRU ordered its residencies in NATO capitals and Japan to scrutinize "all political, military, and intelligence activities that might indicate preparations for mobilization." Were large numbers of soldiers and armed police suddenly appearing in the streets – it was asked – or had the British royal family been moved to a more distant locale?

When the exercises ended nine days later, the acute panic felt by Soviet intelligence subsided only gradually, particularly in light of the cruise and Pershing II missiles that arrived in Britain and West Germany shortly thereafter. For another seven years, the RYAN program continued to collect information that was submitted in a semi-annual report to the Kremlin leadership. The Able Archer scare, however, had a major impact in the West. Even though the CIA badly misread the mindset of the Soviet leadership, seeing merely political posturing at play, a highly regarded asset in the British residency – KGB Colonel Oleg Gordievsky – briefed Prime Minister Margaret Thatcher about the reality of Moscow's "apocalyptic vision." She, in turn, conveyed this information to the United States in an effort to defuse the situation. For Reagan, witnessing the depth of Soviet paranoia sparked a fundamental reorientation in US policy toward the Soviet Union. Not only was a subgroup within the National Security Planning Group expressly charged with calming Soviet fears of a nuclear first strike, but Reagan delivered an unusually conciliatory speech early the following year, urging a "serious" and "constructive" dialogue with Moscow. Following his defection in 1985, Gordievsky met with Reagan in the Oval Office and received the president's personal gratitude for the inside knowledge that he had earlier supplied.

Latin America also returned to the list of foreign policy priorities during the early Reagan administration. In July 1979, the Frente Sandinista de Liberación Nacional (FSLN) or Sandinistas staged a guerilla coup and ousted the weak and corrupt Nicaraguan dictator, Anatasio Somoza. Both the CIA and KGB registered complete surprise at the rapid victory of the Sandinista forces, which had relied heavily on the Cuban DGI for arms and tactical advice. The FSLN rapidly transformed itself into a Marxist-Leninist vanguard party, which, in alliance with Cuba and the Soviet bloc, began to sponsor other guerilla movements in Central America, convinced that armed conflict was the only path to liberation.

The KGB dispatched 70 advisors and established a Nicaraguan school for state security. With the enthusiastic endorsement of Fidel Castro, the next target became the repressive military regime in El Salvador.

The new US president, privy to intelligence detailing Soviet expansionism in the western hemisphere, decided against US military intervention and chose instead the more circumspect policy of covert support for the indigenous resistance to the Sandinistas and the Salvadorian revolutionaries – what one official called the "low-ball option." Congress approved substantial aid packages, including CIA advisors and bases in Honduras and Costa Rica for the anti-Sandinista "Contra" rebels. Contrary to the allegations of the communist Nicaraguan government and its sympathizers, this insurgent army was not an unrepresentative American creation filled with disgruntled ex-Somazista soldiers, but rather the tip of a popular peasant resistance movement based in the rural highlands. By late 1983 these forces had grown to as many as 6,000 fighters – compared to fewer than 1,000 two years earlier – and conducted several major offensives, causing visible concern among the Sandinista army commanders.[5]

Yet Congressional opposition to this covert funding continued to mount. In early 1984, after securing Reagan's approval, the CIA began to place magnetic mines in three of Nicaragua's harbors, primarily to discourage oil shipments and thus cripple the country's economy. Six foreign ships, including a Soviet tanker, were damaged as a result. Even though the Senate Intelligence Committee had been briefed on several prior occasions, a firestorm broke out when news of the CIA's direct involvement appeared in the national press on April 6. The House of Representatives reacted by passing even stricter legislation regarding aid to the Contras – the so-called second Boland Amendment – which denied funds to the CIA, the Defense Department, or any other agency involved in intelligence activities that were earmarked for "military or paramilitary operations in Nicaragua." Duane "Dewey" Clarridge, the talented and flamboyant author of the mining operation, received a new assignment as head of the clandestine service's European division.

Ardently determined to keep the Contras alive as a viable force, the Reagan administration – and DCI Casey, in particular – turned to foreign sources to solicit new funding (Saudi Arabia contributed altogether US$32 million). Responsibility for this covert support also shifted from the CIA to the National Security Council (NSC) and a staff officer, marine Lieutenant Colonel Oliver North. The administration's other immediate foreign preoccupation was the hostage crisis in Lebanon – nine Americans, including the CIA chief of station in Beirut, had been abducted by the pro-Iranian terrorist group Hezbollah. Lured by the possibility of their rescue through an obscure group of Iranian "moderates," Reagan agreed to the sale by Israel of more than 2,000 American anti-tank missiles to Iran, despite its current classification as a state-sponsor of international terrorism. North then devised a plan to divert the profits from the arms sales to Iran to the Contras. To avoid the restrictions of the Boland amendment, he encouraged the formation of a hybrid organization, independent of the government but carrying out covert activities often in cooperation with US officials.

Few parties, it seems, gained from this Iran–Contra imbroglio. William Buckley, the CIA officer, was brutally tortured and killed, and only three of the other hostages were released. The NSC had proven itself amateurish at best in trying to conduct intelligence work on its own (the CIA had been kept largely in the dark, and North later conceded that "I knew nothing about covert operations when I came to the NSC" and "little about Latin America").[6] And by running afoul of the Boland restriction and attempting a cover-up, the Reagan administration was plunged into the worst political crisis since Watergate when the scandal broke into the headlines. Even the Contras received only marginal benefit from the efforts of North and others on their behalf. Although the Sandinistas reaped a considerable propaganda advantage, the Soviet Union increasingly criticized their chronic mismanagement of the country's quasi-command economy and was reluctant to continue its aid program. Fatally miscalculating, the Sandinistas agreed to the peace plan put forward by Oscar Arias Sánchez, the president of Costa Rica, only to be voted out of power by a broad coalition of opposition groups in the internationally supervised elections that followed in February 1990. Humberto Ortega, the Sandinista defense minister, further conceded that arming the Salvadoran guerillas ten years earlier had turned out to be a critical error on their part – one that had extracted a "heavy price."

The terrorist issue, which had bedeviled Europe throughout the 1970s, had by no means disappeared. In the early morning of April 5, 1986, a bomb exploded in the La Belle Discothèque in West Berlin, known to be a popular leisure destination for American military personnel stationed in the city. Two US servicemen and a Turkish woman were killed and more than 200 persons injured. Telex intercepts by the United States confirmed that this act, ordered by Tripoli, had been set in motion by the Libyan embassy (or People's Bureau) in East Berlin. Coupled with recent shootings at the Rome and Vienna airports, this new incident prompted Reagan to order the bombing of military targets in Libya, including the compound of the country's leader, Colonel Muammar al-Qaddafi, regarded by many as the principal sponsor of international terrorism (intelligence reports later characterized him as traumatized by the assault). The United States further charged East Germany and the Soviet Union for having been in a position to prevent this incident but chosen not to do so.

Although Moscow had begun to distance itself from Qaddafi, an earlier intelligence and security agreement had established a working relationship between the two countries. In addition to major arms transactions, the KGB provided training for Libyan intelligence officers at its main facility, the Andropov Institute, while Libya conveyed important information regarding Egypt, Israel, and North Africa. Following the La Belle bombing, East Germany took no action against the personnel of the Libyan residency in East Berlin other than holding "friendly, comradely talks" as ordered by GDR leader Erich Honecker. Not until after reunification did a final legal settlement occur. In 2004, Germany's highest court upheld the conviction of three major figures along with the ruling that assigned responsibility for the discothèque bombing to the Libyan secret service.

The weightiest task of the CIA, however, involved ascertaining the dimensions of the military threat posed by the Soviet Union. In the fall of 1976, the President's Foreign Intelligence Advisory Board became aware of a glaring discrepancy between the agency's assessment and some hard evidence that had reached the board. After its chairman suggested a "competitive analysis," George H. W. Bush, the recently appointed DCI, approved the formation of a "Team B" composed of outside experts who were given access to the same raw data as "Team A" representing the agency. In its starkly pessimistic report, Team B concluded that the Soviets were not committed to a mutual-deterrence, arms-reduction strategy as commonly believed, but were convinced instead that a superior military force could "pressure the West to acquiesce or ... be used to win a military contest at any level."[7] A nuclear war, in other words, was seen as winnable by an ideologically driven adversary. Even though this assessment was strongly challenged by politicians and the media, the CIA began to revise some of its estimates regarding Soviet intentions. Moreover, subsequent directors chose to continue the practice of soliciting advice from experts outside the agency, while members of Team B found influential positions four years later in the Reagan administration, insisting that the United States should press for military superiority, not just parity, in order to achieve a realistic understanding with the Soviets.

Immediately after his confirmation as general secretary in March 1985, Mikhail Gorbachev revealed himself as a new type of Kremlin leader. Foreign observers took note of his relative youth and vigor, his cleverness and agile mind, and even his wit and humor. The Soviet public found him to be their first head of state willing to mingle among them on regular walkabouts, and unlike his immediate predecessors, he had the ability to speak extemporaneously. By April 1986, he had also initiated the withdrawal of Soviet troops from Afghanistan. Still, as the favorite protégé of Andropov, Gorbachev well understood the requisites of exercising power, which included cultivating good relations with the KGB. Its chairman, Viktor Chebrikov, was not only made a Hero of Socialist Labor and a voting member of the Politburo but featured prominently in the Soviet press. One lengthy article of his lauded the successful struggle waged against Western intelligence agencies and rejected the "slanderous allegations" of "bourgeois propagandists" concerning human rights violations.[8] With the assistance of the security forces, Gorbachev also proceeded to purge many of the Brezhnev old guard under the rubric of an anticorruption campaign. Significantly, too, the public image of the new Soviet leader – strikingly projected on state television – was carefully coordinated with the help of the KGB.

Nevertheless, the important role played by *aktiviniie meropriatia* (or active measures) showed few signs of diminishment. Its institutional origins can be traced to 1969, when a special unit was established within the KGB to produce and disseminate black propaganda and disinformation for the purpose of influencing international opinion, especially in the Third World, and sowing mistrust in the Western alliance. About 10 to 15 forgeries of US government documents were produced annually. One of the most successful active measures of the early Gorbachev years sought to blame the AIDS epidemic on American biological warfare, alleging that the virus had been "manufactured" during genetic engineering experiments at Fort Detrick, Maryland, and spread through the world by US servicemen who had been used as guinea pigs. Spain, Greece, Turkey, and the United Kingdom counted among the key targets, since they were all considering placing restrictions on the US military presence in their countries. Another fabricated but effective active measure charged the United States with butchering Latin American babies and using their bodies for organ parts. This story became extensively publicized in the press of more than 50 countries and even reached the pages of the worldwide magazine of the Jehovah's Witnesses.

Upon embarking on his program of *perestroika* (or restructuring), Gorbachev regarded the KGB as a major asset in acquiring vital Western scientific and technological knowledge. Within the First Chief Directorate, it was Directorate T, composed almost exclusively of persons with a scientific and engineering background, that specialized in this form of espionage – assisted to a large degree by the allied services of Czechoslovakia and East Germany. Not surprisingly, expanded intelligence-gathering in the military field stood at the top of the agenda. By the end of the Gorbachev era – according to one estimate – roughly 150 Soviet weapons systems were derived from technology stolen from the West.

In contrast, Gorbachev's other principal reform – *glasnost* (or openness) – caused considerable unease within the security forces. Prompted by the Chernobyl nuclear reactor disaster in April 1986, it called for a freer investigation of the Soviet past as well as greater transparency regarding current political, social, and economic conditions. The KGB itself was publicly called to account the following year by *Pravda* for the unlawful arrest of a journalist on fraudulent charges of "hooliganism." In Chebrikov's view, however, the Western intelligence services were simply manipulating this liberalized environment in order to advance their "ideological subversion." During the summer of 1988, Gorbachev attempted a major overhaul of the decision-making process, shifting more power to the government bureaucracy at the expense of the party apparatus. As far as the KGB was concerned, Chebrikov was replaced by Vladimir Kryuchkov – another protégé of Andropov (dating from the Hungarian Revolution) as well as the first head of the foreign intelligence directorate ever to ascend to this position. Retaining his status as a full member of the Politburo, Chebrikov was not consigned to political oblivion but managed to exercise major behind-the-scenes influence on security policy for more than a year. Gorbachev's unwillingness to subject the KGB to any legal controls further reflected his fundamental ambivalence toward the still powerful institution.

As chairman of the KGB, Kryuchkov promptly embarked on an unprecedented public relations campaign to foster the impression of an upright, law-abiding institution. "Violence, inhumanity, and the violation of human rights have always been alien to the work of our secret services," he stated to the Italian paper *L'Unità*. The press was also invited to the Foreign Ministry to view a film documentary on the "new KGB," which conspicuously sought to humanize the personnel of the security apparatus. In a remarkable reversal, the Western services, only recently depicted as implacable antagonists, now merited favorable comparisons. The Eighth Chief Directorate for cryptography, as an example, was likened publicly to the US National Security Agency. Probably the campaign's most novel innovation was the selection of Katya Mayorova as "Miss KGB." In announcing the holder of the world's only "security services beauty title," the mass-circulation broadsheet daily *Komsomolskaya Pravda* stressed not only the woman's attractiveness but her ability to "deliver a karate kick to her enemy's head."[9]

Unbeknownst to the outside world, however, the KGB had only recently gained one of its most valuable double agents of the Cold War. Frustrated by his slow erratic career advancement and yearning for a more affluent lifestyle for himself and his Columbian-born wife, Aldrich Ames, a senior counterintelligence officer in the CIA's Soviet division, volunteered his services to the Soviet *rezidenz* in Washington in April 1985. What he had intended merely as a devious scheme – providing the names of agents he believed were already known by the KGB – soon turned into a far graver matter. Within two months – encouraged by his skillful handler Victor Cherkashin – Ames (code name LYUDMILA) had divulged the names of more than 20 Western agents. Two managed to escape Soviet authorities, notably Oleg Gordievsky, the newly designated resident in London and a British collaborator since 1974, but the majority were summarily executed. The biggest loss was a high-ranking officer in the KGB's North American counterintelligence section codenamed G. T. PROLOGUE.

Ames further provided CIA documents and cables that revealed its complete *modus operandi* in the Soviet Union. Such knowledge then enabled the Soviets to run a number of successful double-agent operations against the United States. By the time of his arrest nine years later, the KGB and its successor agency had paid him US$2.7 million. Ames's full cooperation with American authorities prevented his own execution and resulted in a life sentence. From Moscow's perspective – according to Cherkashin – Ames's efforts were considered "worth every penny" of this seemingly unprecedented sum.[10] The CIA, by contrast, regarded his treason as undoubtedly the greatest counterintelligence failure in its history.

At the same time, the KGB could take little comfort in recent developments in the Eastern bloc, especially in Poland. Despite the skillful imposition of martial law and suppression of Solidarity, Jaruzelski's regime had obtained only a temporary respite. In June 1983, John Paul returned to his homeland for a second time, attracting vast throngs again at every juncture and urging those imprisoned and persecuted by the government to find spiritual refuge in the church. In the eyes of the KGB, Jaruzelski himself came under increasing suspicion, not only because of his decision to terminate martial law a month after the pope's visit but also owing to his tolerance of officials with dangerous revisionist views in his entourage.

The following year the regime suffered another severe blow when several members of the SB religious-affairs department abducted and murdered a pro-Solidarity priest, Father Jerzy Popieluszko – described by Wałesa as the "unofficial chaplain" of the movement. Sensing the widespread popular outrage as nearly one million mourners streamed to his funeral, Jaruzelski tried to disavow any connection with his government by taking the unusual step of ordering a public trial of the murderers – a move that further disquieted the Soviet security forces. The four SB officers received prison terms ranging from 14 to 25 years, which were later drastically reduced for unexplained reasons. The CIA responded to the cleric's death by printing his photograph on 40,000 postcards along with texts from some of his sermons and smuggling them into the country.

With more storm clouds gathering on the horizon, a meeting of the Soviet bloc intelligence services convened in East Berlin in October 1988. The bleak uncertainty of the future dominated the proceedings and was reflected in the fact that, for the first time, those attending left the date and location of the next meeting undetermined. The concluding evening featured a boat excursion along the city's extensive waterways. Vadim Kirpichenko, the first deputy head of Soviet foreign intelligence, recalled the melancholy mood of the occasion: "In many cases, one was saying farewell forever. The commonwealth of intelligence services of the socialist countries had ended its existence."[11]

Clearly East Germany – Moscow's most important and productive Warsaw Pact ally – faced mounting domestic opposition. In addition to ever larger numbers requesting exit visas, spontaneous, but peaceful, demonstrations began to take place in the major cities, sparked by the exposure of recent electoral manipulation. Longtime Stasi chief Erich Mielke reacted in his accustomed manner and angrily told Leonid Shebarshin, the new head of the KGB's first directorate, that "in the exercise of power, there are no concessions to be made – neither to the imperialist opponents nor to the hostile, oppositional domestic forces."[12] Emphatically resisting the Gorbachev reform program – *glasnost*, in particular – the East German leadership under Honecker looked favorably at the example of Chinese authorities who had exercised deadly force in the Tiananmen Square massacre. In October 1989, following the ceremonies marking the fortieth anniversary of the founding of the GDR, the police took to nightsticks and water cannons and dragged thousands to jail, but to no avail. With chants of "Out with the Stasi," the security forces now found themselves the focal point of popular discontent, as the protests, spearheaded by the Monday night "demos" in Leipzig, continued to gain momentum throughout the country.

In the meanwhile, a substantial West German sum offered to the reform-minded communist government of Hungary to assist in covering its budget deficit helped to secure the opening of its borders. That move made it possible for East Germans to flee to the Federal

Republic via Austria. As a result, tens of thousands of GDR citizens rushed to Prague and Budapest and found temporary refuge in the West German embassies there. Moscow remained conspicuously silent, thereby signaling its increasing non-involvement in Central and Eastern Europe during these critical months (Gorbachev later claimed that, by this time, he was prepared to withdraw all Soviet military forces from the region). The "active measures" that had been designed by the KGB to aid the Eastern bloc communist leaders never found implementation. "They were educated only to be friends of the Soviet Union," Sherbarshin complained. "They were never prepared to stand on their own feet."[13]

Neither the resignation of Honecker in favor of Egon Krenz, the party's ambitious "crown prince," nor the ignominious departure of Mielke from his post following a desperate speech before the People's Chamber succeeded in stabilizing the East German situation. With the Berlin Wall now open – an event which no one on either side had foreseen – the Stasi made one final attempt at survival. In mid-November, it transformed itself into the Office for National Security (Amt für Nationale Sicherheit, or AfNS) with Wolfgang Schwanitz, a former deputy minister, as its head. Nothing in this loyal bureaucrat's résumé suggested that he would inspire the younger generation of Stasi officers, let alone the population at large (the AfNS soon acquired the nickname "Nasi"). Failing to recognize the growing hostility directed at the so-called *inoffizielle Mitarbeiter* (unofficial collaborators) – the massive group of informers skillfully recruited over the years – he announced at a top-level staff meeting that they must be reactivated "in strictest secrecy."

Schwanitz also intensified Operation REISSWOLF (or Shredder) – the action initiated by Mielke to destroy all incriminating evidence ranging from the evaluations of informer reports to the lists of reserve cadres. A supplemental order stated that highly sensitive material was to be transferred from the county offices to the appropriate district office; the most important items were then to be transported to the main headquarters. In early December, the KGB dispatched a special commission to East Berlin demanding that all documents of operational interest be collected within a week and sent to Moscow; items of lesser significance were simply destroyed at a Red Army facility using a flame thrower. At that point, the tight relationship that had existed between the KGB and the MfS for nearly 40 years effectively ended.

Even though Schwanitz had specified that REISSWOLF proceed in a "very intelligent and inconspicuous manner," citizens' groups spontaneously formed to protest the destruction of these records. In early December – after seeing several days of black smoke billowing from the interior court of the Stasi district office – the local citizens' group in

Erfurt chose to occupy the premises. This example spread rapidly throughout the GDR and explains why so many documents managed to survive. By contrast, the foreign intelligence division in East Berlin proceeded unhindered and left hardly a trace behind. According to its last director, Werner Grossmann, the shredders operated around the clock and had to be refrigerated occasionally to prevent overheating.

With the continuing occupation of the regional offices by the citizens' committees and the emergence of the Central Roundtable calling for its dissolution, the AfNS was officially disbanded in mid-December. Could a bolder reform plan have averted this outcome? The most credible alternative was offered by Markus Wolf, the accomplished former head of the foreign intelligence branch who still enjoyed considerable popularity within the security forces (he was also the only Stasi official – past or present – who elected to speak at one of the mass November demonstrations). While critical of Mielke's dogmatic doctrine of total surveillance, he still held to the glorified image of Dzerzhinsky's Cheka, ignoring the brutal terror unleashed by the early Bolsheviks and making no mention of any legal safeguards for the future.[14] In any event, Wolf's plan never moved beyond some preliminary discussions.

A closer look at these critical months reveals a series of fatal fissures that occurred. Within the Stasi, the local and district offices felt increasingly estranged from the East Berlin headquarters, just as younger officers were often at odds with their senior comrades. There further existed no cohesion with the People's Police or the Combat Groups of the Working Class. Most serious of all were the mutual recriminations between officials of the party and the security forces, each finding the other largely to blame for the current dilemma. That the Soviet Union decided to assume a passive role had a profound impact as well. As Grossmann lamented, "For us it was bitter to be left in the lurch by our 'Soviet friends' in Moscow."[15]

As the hemorrhaging of the GDR was taking place, the CIA felt acute consternation. Over the years, East German counterintelligence had thoroughly neutralized all of the human assets recruited by the United States. Wolf's superiors, at one point, had worried that the GDR was not being taken seriously by the Americans because of their "haphazard" methods. This meant that the CIA possessed no means of gaining insight into the daily decision-making of the communist regime at this critical juncture. Reduced to the role of a simple spectator, Richard Rolph, the East Berlin station chief, found himself and his wife joining the joyful surging crowds on the evening the Berlin Wall was inadvertently opened. The cable that he promptly sent his superiors merely confirmed the free passage at the newly opened checkpoints into West

Berlin. Filling this information void for officials in Washington was the extensive televised coverage provided by CNN. Strikingly, this episode marked the beginning of an unspoken competition between the cable network and the CIA during the final years of the Cold War. According to one knowledgeable source, "Headquarters repeatedly told case officers not to try to match everything on the news and instead to focus on stealing secrets that President couldn't find out about anywhere else."[16]

In Czechoslovakia, the so-called "Velvet Revolution" led by Vaclav Havel was characterized by its relatively short duration – roughly ten days – as well as by the buoyant mood among its supporters who incorporated rock music, wit, and even some absurdity into their cause. The choice of the basement of Prague's Laterna Magika (or Magic Lantern Theater) as Havel's informal headquarters seemed altogether in keeping with this spirit. Initially, the StB (or Czechoslovakian secret service) thought that the country's relatively high living standards would shield it from the unrest elsewhere in the Eastern bloc, but the fall of the Berlin Wall shattered that illusion.

After a tumultuous confrontation in Prague between riot police and student protesters in mid-November, the head of the StB, Alojz Lorenc, became convinced that his organization could only survive in a reformed communist state. He therefore sought to manipulate the rapidly unfolding situation by having government hardliners replaced with Gorbachev-style politicians. Codenamed WEDGE, the operation further sought to infiltrate the dissident movement with informers and had even selected a candidate, Zdenek Mlynar, to assume the leadership of the country. Yet these elaborate schemes quickly faltered. Mlynar, living in exile in Vienna, showed no interest at all.

With the formation of Havel's Civic Forum later that month, Lorenc, a careerist above all else, entered into secret negotiations to try to escape prosecution. In addition – to bolster his new image as a reformer – he appeared at a mass demonstration in Letna Park but found himself loudly rebuffed when his speech began to lapse into familiar Marxist-Leninist formulations. Even so, the leaders of Civic Forum acted slowly before eventually dissolving the StB. Lorenc remained in office until his dismissal on December 21. By that time, one third of the organization's files, at his direction, had either been destroyed or otherwise disappeared.

Of the Eastern bloc states, Romania alone saw the escalation of its revolution into open violence, ultimately resulting in more than 1,000 deaths on both sides of the conflict. Beginning in Timisoara, large-scale protests against the brutal regime of Nicolae Ceauşescu spread to several other cities including Bucharest. On December 22, confronted by a jeering crowd in Palace Square, the Conducător and his wife Elena fled the capital by helicopter but were later captured, tried by an improvised military court, and executed by a firing squad on Christmas Day. In seeking to avert this outcome, Securitate troops and police units had taken on the role of snipers, firing at civilian and army targets and seeking to thwart the efforts of the National Salvation Front, the fledgling revolutionary government. The head of the Securitate, Colonel-General Iulian Vlad, assumed an ambiguous stance toward the intensifying conflict. Initially accepted by the inner circle of the National Salvation Front as an unlikely convert, he stubbornly refused to call upon those under his command to cease fighting and lay down their arms. Increasingly, Vlad's profession of loyalty to the revolution rang hollow to the leadership, and he was belatedly arrested and charged with "complicity to genocide."

As centrifugal forces began to develop in the Soviet Union declaring independence from Moscow's rule, Gorbachev faced a growing dilemma. Whereas he was able to assert that the Eastern bloc states were essentially on their own and would not suffer military reprisals, there loomed the acute danger of the USSR's own disintegration. In Lithuania, for example, the KGB and the army had been running operations designed to intimidate the popularly elected government for more than a year. In January 1990, an attempt to install a puppet regime – the National Salvation Committee – resulted in a violent clash with demonstrators at the Vilnius television tower; at least 14 people were killed and hundreds injured. This clumsily executed coup failed in the end, embittering the population even more but also disillusioning those liberal supporters of Gorbachev who still believed in a reformed Communist Party.

By the end of the year, the Soviet leader had turned sharply to the right by appointing a cabinet filled with hardliners determined to quell the restive republics and maintain strict party control in the state. As Kryuchkov told former President Richard Nixon at a meeting in Moscow, "We have had about as much democracy as we can stomach."[17] Sensing a growing defeatism in his own organization, the KGB chairman responded by setting up a special unit – described as an "analytical center" – to try to bolster morale among the rank-and-file. Nikolai Leonov, one of the most successful First Chief Directorate officers in the Third World, was recalled to head an anti-Western propaganda campaign based less on Marxist-Leninist ideology than on an outright appeal to Russian patriotism. In another ominous move, Kryuchkov ordered service weapons to be issued once again, reversing a decision made under Brezhnev to disarm KGB officers on the domestic front.

Another complicating factor was the political comeback of Boris Yeltsin, who had been ousted as Moscow party chief in 1987 for advocating reforms deemed too radical. His election in spring 1990 as chairman of the Russian Supreme Soviet had been vigorously opposed by Gorbachev, whose prestige dropped even further as a consequence. A pessimistic CIA assessment at the time noted the Soviet leader's loss of control over the political process and raised the possibility of a coup attempt. As the Soviet republics continued their quest for more autonomy – among those declaring their sovereignty were Russia, Uzbekistan, Moldavia, Georgia, Ukraine, and Belarus – Gorbachev put forth a union plan that sought to save the federation by making serious concessions in the areas of defense, foreign relations, and the budget. Although boycotted in several of the republics, a referendum held in mid-March 1991 showed a wide margin of support for the plan. Two months later a CIA paper to President George Bush and his senior advisors struck an even bleaker tone regarding Gorbachev's plummeting credibility at home and the survival of "the current center-dominated political system."[18] Bush attempted to alert the Soviet leader about the coup preparations via Jack Matlock, the US ambassador in Moscow, but his warning made no impact at all.

The "emergency committee" that had formed was headed by Kryuchkov and included seven other members of the inner circle, notably the defense and interior ministers. Already unsettled by Yeltsin's election in June as president of Russia, they were determined to act prior to the formal signing of the Union Treaty scheduled for August 20. While vacationing at his Black Sea dacha at Foros, Gorbachev – according to his recollection – reluctantly received four emissaries accompanied by the chief of the KGB Guard regiment on August 19. His refusal to accede to their demands resulted in his house arrest under heavy surveillance for the next 72 hours. Telephone lines, he further alleged, had been cut to prevent contacting anyone outside of Foros. The accuracy of this version has not gone unchallenged.[19] Among numerous discrepancies is the fact that Gorbachev made telephone calls to one of his allies during the purported communications blackout. Likewise, it seems implausible that such a shrewd politician had no inkling of his trusted colleague's scheme and that no attempt was made by the 32 personal guards to come to the aid of their leader. Contrary to the commonly accepted account, such evidence suggests that Gorbachev, far from being a hapless victim in this episode, had found common cause with the conspirators' plan to put the treaty signing on hold and declare a state of emergency.

Whatever his motives, Gorbachev, back in Moscow, lost further ground to Yeltsin by resigning his position as general secretary while still affirming his communist allegiance. By that time his archrival had become the undisputed rallying point for advocates of democratic change. The ill-conceived coup, publicly condemned by the Bush administration as illegitimate and unconstitutional, also collapsed within days. Although Yeltsin and his entourage had expected a storming of the Russian White House (or parliament building) by the KGB's elite "Alpha" special operations unit, no orders were issued and it never occurred. Through intercepted messages, US signals intelligence found little support for the coup within the military. Utterly unrepentant, Kryuchkov, along with 14 other men associated with the conspiracy, was apprehended and charged with treason. Yeltsin moved swiftly to consolidate his newfound power. The Communist Party was banned, and he took control of key institutions such as the State Bank and Finance Ministry.

In the eyes of the democratic opposition, the KGB, even more than the party, embodied the unbridled tyranny of Soviet rule. Easily the most evocative scene of all during this turbulent period occurred on the evening of August 22 when large crowds gathered outside KGB headquarters in Moscow. Some of the protesters threatened to enter the Lubyanka. But the main focus of attention was the imposing 15-ton bronze statue of Feliks Dzerzhinsky that stood outside. Begun in earnest under Khrushchev, the veneration of Lenin's first security chief had found expression in countless forms – from renamed streets and squares throughout the USSR to miniature bronze replicas of him that tourists could purchase at the GUM department store across from Lenin's tomb. To topple this largest representation of all – erected in 1958 – thus held unusual symbolic significance.

Thousands of Muscovites stayed late in the night until "Iron Feliks" was finally removed from its pedestal with the aid of a heavy German-made crane. A volunteer had climbed atop Dzerzhinsky's shoulders and placed the crane's iron cable around his neck in the manner of an execution. The statue was subsequently transported to a makeshift graveyard of fallen Soviet heroes near Gorky Park, and Lubyanka Square regained its original name. Skeptics, however, wondered whether these events represented a culminating moment or just an interlude in the long history of the KGB.

Notes

1 Cited by Victor Sebestyen, *Revolution 1989: The Fall of the Soviet Empire* (New York, NY: Pantheon, 2009), 22.
2 Cited by John Lewis Gaddis, *The Cold War: A New History* (London: Penguin), 219.

3 Robert M. Gates, *From the Shadows: The Ultimate Insider's Story of Five Presidents and How They Won the Cold War* (New York, NY: Simon and Schuster, 1996), 356.

4 Cited by Alexander Dallin, *Black Box: KAL 007 and the Superpowers* (Berkeley, CA: University of California Press, 1985), 15.

5 See Timothy C. Brown, *The Real Contra War: Highlander Peasant Resistance in Nicaragua* (Norman, OK: University of Oklahoma Press, 2001).

6 Oliver L. North (with William Novak), *Under Fire: An American Story* (New York, NY: HarperCollins, 1991), 180, 223.

7 The executive summary of the Team B report can be found at http://neoconservatism.vaisse.net/doku.php?id=report_of_team_b.

8 Cited by Amy W. Knight, *The KGB: Police and Politics in the Soviet Union* (Boston, MA: Allen & Unwin, 1988), 98.

9 Cited by David Remnick, *Lenin's Tomb: The Last Days of the Soviet Empire* (New York, NY: Random House, 1993), 342–343.

10 Victor Cherkashin (with Gregory Feifer), *Spy Handler: Memoir of a KGB Officer* (New York, NY: Basic Books, 2005), 4.

11 Christopher Andrew and Vasili Mitrokhin, *The World was Going Our Way: The KGB and the Battle for the Third World* (New York, NY: Basic Books, 2005), 476.

12 "Erich Mielke (MfS) und Leonid Schebarschin (KGB) über den drohenen Untergang des Sozialistischen Lagers. Protokoll eines Streitgesprächs vom 7 April 1989," in Walter Süß (Ed.), *Deutschland Archiv*, September 1993, 1033.

13 Cited by Christopher Andrew, "KGB Foreign Intelligence from Brezhnev to the Coup," in *Intelligence and National Security*, 8(3) (1993), 63.

14 Markus Wolf, *Im eigenen Auftrag: Bekenntnisse und Einsichten* (Munich: Schneekluth Verlag, 1991).

15 Werner Großmann, *Bonn im Blick: Die DDR-Aufklärung aus der Sicht ihres letzten Chefs* (Berlin: Das Neue Berlin, 2001), 208.

16 Milt Bearden and James Risen, *The Main Enemy: The Inside Story of the CIA's Final Showdown with the KGB* (New York, NY: Random House, 2003), 397.

17 Remnick, *Lenin's Tomb*, 398.

18 Gates, *From the Shadows*, 520.

19 See John B. Dunlop, *The Rise of Russia and the Fall of the Soviet Empire* (Princeton, NJ: Princeton University Press, 1995), 202–206; and Amy Knight, *Spies Without Cloaks: The KGB's Successors* (Princeton, NJ: Princeton University Press, 1996), 17–28.

8 The Aftermath

Germany's preoccupation with the Stasi phenomenon hardly ended with the fall of the Berlin Wall. On January 15, 1990, a large angry crowd assembled in front of the sprawling state security complex on the Normannenstrasse in East Berlin. Once inside, the demonstrators laid waste to many of the offices, tearing the pictures of ex-GDR leader Erich Honecker from the walls and wrecking much of the furniture. Although the precise origin of this raucous event remains unclarified, its larger meaning was captured by a hand-printed cloth banner unfurled from an upper-story window: "Occupied: the files belong to us." A central "Citizens Committee Normannenstrasse" consequently formed in order to make certain that the Stasi and its successor agency had been completely dissolved and its records preserved.

A heated debate soon ensued. Some argued for the destruction of the files, predicting "murder and mayhem" if they were to be used to determine the culpability of Stasi collaborators. Others proposed locking the documents away for 50 years and then opening them. Western intelligence agencies chafed at having the clandestine practices of the security services exposed to public view. Yet, by August the East German parliament had passed the "Law on the Securing and Use of Individual-Based Data of the former Ministry for State Security/Office for National Security." Most significantly, it established the basic principles that were incorporated in the Stasi files legislation following unification – that the files remain in the territory of the former GDR independent of any political party or ministry and that individual citizens have the right to inspect their own file.

The government agency placed in charge bore the unwieldy title of the Federal Commissioner for the Records of the State Security Service of the former German Democratic Republic (BStU), which became better known as the Gauck Authority after its first director, Joachim Gauck. A dissident Lutheran minister from Rostock (and later president of the FRG), he stated that "the most crucial decision for us East Germans is whether we have the strength and self-confidence, not to walk away from our history, but to confront its good and bad sides."[1] As an administrative body, the BStU was charged with providing government agencies and private corporations with relevant data but could not make any recommendations regarding dismissals. It also established a careful procedure that allowed individuals to inspect their files (the names of third persons, for example, were blacked out). By the end of 2006, more than 6 million persons – East and West Germans as well as many foreigners – had submitted an application. A survey conducted several years earlier indicated overwhelming satisfaction by those who had undergone this historically unprecedented experience.

Denunciations of MfS head Erich Mielke began as soon as he lost power. Despite a long list of charges by state prosecutors, the presiding judge in Berlin declared him unfit to stand trial for reasons of health. They then pursued another tact – holding Mielke responsible for the murder of two Berlin policemen in 1931 – and obtained permission for Mielke's limited participation. In 1993, he received a six-year prison term but was released two years later to a nursing home. The other major East German intelligence official facing prosecution was Markus Wolf (he had declined an earlier CIA offer of money, plastic surgery, and relocation to California in exchange for specific information). Yet, in this unchartered legal territory, it was unclear whether he could be charged with espionage committed in the FRG while based in the GDR. The first trial, despite a guilty verdict, was overturned by Germany's highest court in Karlsruhe. In a second trial – by focusing on kidnappings rather than espionage – state prosecutors obtained only a two-year suspended sentence. Whereas soldiers who had served in the East German army were readily absorbed by the Bundeswehr, former Stasi officers found themselves strictly banned from the security services in a united Germany; even ex-support personnel faced formidable obstacles finding a new position in the public sector.

The other country at the forefront of examining the legacy of its security organs was Czechoslovakia. Because of several scandals that accompanied the early screenings for StB connections, the Federal Assembly passed the so-called Lustration Law in October 1991 (the term derives from the Latin word *lustratio* or "purification by sacrifice"). It applied to persons in a range of categories – from knowing StB collaborators to students at KGB schools for more than three months to owners of StB safe houses. Instead of criminal prosecution, they faced a five-year ban from most government-related and military positions but not, curiously, from running for parliament. In defending this highly controversial legislation, its proponents appeared less concerned with exacting retribution than with promoting national security and trust in future democratic governments. Those opposing lustration nevertheless called it an "inquisition" and a form of "legal violence." To some, it seemed grimly reminiscent of the phenomenon of "class guilt" during Stalinist times. President Vaclav Havel sought passage of an amendment to guard against any collective stigma, but most legislators showed little inclination to follow his lead.

After the federation split into the independent states of the Czech Republic and Slovakia in January 1993, the fault lines acquired even greater definition. Much less critical of their communist past, Slovakians resisted the implementation of the Lustration Law and declined to renew it at the end of its five-year life span. By contrast, it was extended twice by the Czech Republic's legislature, on both occasions overriding Havel's veto. From the time that the law took effect until late 2005, the Ministry of the Interior issued 451,000 lustration certificates with only 2.03 percent registering a past collaboration (its extent was not measured).[2] The Czech Republic also allowed its citizens greater access to StB files – four million computerized pages were placed in a repository in the eastern Bohemian town of Pardubice – and attempted to prosecute more members of the former communist regime. In October 1992, a Higher Military Court had found Alojz Lorenc, the last head of the StB, guilty of abuse of power by a public official, but after the split, he escaped to his native Slovakia and received only a 15-month suspended sentence.

In both states, new intelligence organizations arose. Apart from two services attached to the military, the Czech Republic saw the creation of the Bezpečnostní informační služba (Security Information Service, or BIS) and the Úřad pro zahraniční styky a informace (Bureau for Foreign Contacts and Information, or ÚZSI). A remark attributed to Prime Minister Vaclav Klaus in 1994 – "I don't need intelligence services. CNN is enough for me." – was indicative of the center-right government's minimalist approach and desire to keep secret agencies on the periphery of society, not at the center as was the case prior to 1989.[3] Charged with domestic counterintelligence, the BIS focused especially on foreign espionage activity, the greatest threat to the country's stability in its estimation. Among its publicized successes during the mid-1990s was the interception of an illegal shipment of Czech weapons to Iran and Bosnia and three kilos of enriched Soviet uranium-235. The BIS also raided the Russian mafiosi in a Prague restaurant during a deep surveillance operation. The agency simultaneously incurred extensive criticism concerning its own security measures, its fractured relations with the government, and its rapid turnover of staff.

Located in the Prague district of Kobylisy, ÚZSI, the foreign intelligence service, began its operations largely on the basis of open sources and a fresh staff. Its initial director was Oldrich Cerny, a longtime dissident friend of Havel previously active in the film industry. A firm Anglophile as well, he turned to the British to help compensate for his inexperience in this realm and developed a close relationship with the director-general of MI6. The new intelligence officers received field training from the British, and the CIA agreed to supply up-to-date communications equipment. When Britain and the United States asked the Havel government to recall several StB illegals living in their countries, their resistance to leaving caused the plan to be dropped. Having never been activated during their long period abroad, these sleeper agents – Czech authorities reasoned – had inflicted no damage.

Slovakia decided to move in a radically different direction. It established a single institution – the Slovenská informačná služba (Slovak Information Service, or SIS) – which soon acquired the traits of a political police force in the service of the autocratic prime minister, Vladimir Meciar. One of the SIS directors, Ivan Lexa, was the son of a former communist minister and an StB collaborator like his father. During his tenure, not only did intelligence relations with NATO members come asunder but Russia emerged as SIS's principal foreign ally. According to a formal understanding, the Russians provided training for SIS officers at its own facilities as well as in Slovakia. In the mid-1990s, one operation, in particular, sought to strengthen Russian influence among the Slovakian public, while others attempted to sow discord in neighboring lands.

Probably the most bizarre SIS undertaking was the forcible abduction of the son of Slovakian president Michal Kovac – a political rival of Meciar. Left bruised and unconscious in his own car near an Austrian police station, Kovac, Jr. survived the ordeal, and his father refused to abdicate. Meciar's government countered with the contrived accusation of a self-abduction. The solid opposition victory in the general election of 1998 finally resulted in the removal of Lexa and Meciar from office and tentatively inaugurated a long overdue reform of SIS. Some observers were reminded of the events of 1989, as the departing officers – many of them veterans of the StB – immediately resorted to the wholesale destruction of their files.

With the electoral defeat of the Polish Communist Party in mid-1989 began the disintegration of its security service, the SB. In April the following year, the Solidarity-dominated parliament approved the creation of a new agency – Urzad Ochrony Panstwa (State Protection Office, or UOP) – which took possession of its predecessor's files and other property. In a unique arrangement, former SB personnel could be rehired if they passed a verification procedure administered on a district basis. At issue was whether they had violated the law, abused human rights, or sought private gain from their position. Approximately 4,000 of the applicants found their way into the UOP, despite complaints about the lack of uniform standards among the local examining boards. Further screening was ruled out for fear of losing seasoned professionals. Prohibited from monitoring opposition political groups and requiring court approval for a surveillance operation, the UOP had as its principal mission combating terrorism and organized crime.

The Polish government's outright rejection of lustration came under increasing criticism, but attempts to forge a workable policy repeatedly ended in stalemate. Finally, in 1997, a law was passed whereby all ranking elected state officials, members of the judiciary, and mass media leaders had to declare publicly any instance of personal SB collaboration between 1944 and 1990. Only a false statement, which was determined by a lustration court with access to the UOP archives, carried the penalty of a ten-year professional ban. Out of roughly 23,000 people, no more than several dozen were found to have made untruthful submissions. A more stringent revision of the Lustration Law passed in 2006 was struck down by the Constitutional Court the following year. In addition, ordinary Poles, unless expressly victims of communist rule, were denied access to the limited number of SB files that survived.

Hungary's slow, negotiated exit from communist rule set the tone for what followed after 1990. No agreement had been reached beforehand during the roundtable talks with the ruling party about a successor to the AVH, the communist security apparatus. It soon became apparent, however, that it had not mended its old ways and was continuing to collect information on opposition groups perceived as "hostile," despite constitutional changes affirming a multi-party system. Yet, this revelation – known as "Dumagate" – led merely to the elimination of the department charged with domestic repression (Main Division III/III), and the rest of the organization remained intact. Finally, in 1995, legislation put two new civilian bodies in place charged with national security: the Nemzetbiztonsagi Hivatal (National Security Office, or NBH) and the Nemzetbiztonsagi Szakszolgalat (National Security Service, or NBSzSz). According to the division of labor, the former assumed responsibility for gathering and processing both foreign and domestic intelligence, and the latter provided protection within the country's borders and for government officials at home and abroad.

Much of the same pattern appeared in Hungary's approach to lustration. Consensus about how to proceed eluded the loose coalition of opposition parties that had emerged from the 1990 general election. Not until four years later did a belated and heavily diluted lustration law pass the unicameral legislature. According to its provisions, public officials who had sworn an oath before parliament or the president were subjected to a screening based on the archives of the former secret service. If found to have been a collaborator with the AVH – or a member of the fascist Arrow Cross Party – that person had the option of quietly resigning without the stigma of public disclosure. No provision was made for an unmasked official to be removed from office.

This limited transparency reflected the general mood of the country, which preferred to leave the recent past unexamined and seek greater economic prosperity instead. Nevertheless, a heated controversy arose in 2002 when the newly elected socialist premier, Peter Medgyessy, was denounced as a communist-era spy by a leading conservative daily. Promptly confirming the charge, he maintained that his work in the counterintelligence division in the years 1977–1982 had actually benefited the country by preventing "foreign spies from getting their hands on Hungarian secrets" and ensuring "that they should not be able to block us from joining the IMF [International Monetary Fund]."[4] Since the lustration law applied only to collaboration with Main Division III/III, he had not technically violated his oath. But Medgyessy's assertion that his efforts were directed against the Soviet Union, not the West, was refuted by his former case officer, and a public opinion poll showed a substantial majority favoring the premier's departure from office. The opposition, however, failed to garner sufficient support for a no-confidence vote, and no action was taken.

In Bulgaria, too, the transition years did not favor a frank inquiry into the transgressions of the communist period. Political turmoil led to a succession of weak governments and thwarted early attempts at lustration. Widespread mistrust grew in the population, as many saw evidence that the disbanded state security apparatus had not been truly depoliticized. Moreover, utilizing its network of contacts and store of specialized knowledge, its former officers began to find lucrative positions in the private sector – either by launching their own firms or joining those established by ex-communist apparatchiks – and to form close ties with organized crime. Fueling further suspicions among the Bulgarian citizenry was an oddly reserved process, whereby the secret files were opened only after a government-appointed commission had implemented partial lustration without making known its rationale.

That no other Eastern European country possessed a higher percentage of communist party members relative to the total population posed added difficulties for Romania following its violent revolution in 1989. Remaining fundamentally unreconstructed, many merely joined the ruling National Salvation Front. Eleven generals from the Securitate and the militia were eventually placed on trial for their attempted suppression of the revolution; but in the case of Iulian Vlad, the former Securitate head, his nine-year prison sentence ended in 1994 with early parole. Given the preeminent role played by the security agency in the conduct of foreign trade, ex-Securitate officers, like their colleagues in Bulgaria, had little difficulty in deeply penetrating the private sector. In addition, they came to occupy key positions in the government administration, notably as diplomats and members of the Ministry of Trade.

With the dissolution of the Securitate in early 1990 came the creation of a new security and intelligence structure – nine different agencies each built around the nucleus of a former directorate or unit. For many Romanians, this fragmentation spelled little change and seemed essentially a ploy to project a more democratic facade to foreigners and thus enhance the country's chances of admission to the European Union and NATO. The largest of the new agencies was the Serviciul Roman de Informatii (Romanian Security Service, or SRI), whose director struggled to craft a fresh image in spite of infighting, several scandals, and the continued presence of a number of ex-Securitate officers. Foreign intelligence came under the purview of the SRI. In a well-publicized instance of post-Cold War intelligence cooperation with the West, Major-General Mihai Caraman, the first head of the SRI, provided the French security service with a copy of a dossier involving a former socialist defense minister, Charles Hernu. A regular paid informant of the Bulgarian DS and the KGB, Hernu (code name ANDRE) was the first cabinet-level officer in a Western democracy exposed as an earlier Eastern bloc agent.

Yet, the largest question of all centered on the fate of the KGB following the collapse of the hardline coup of August 1991. The next four months saw a struggle between the forces of Gorbachev and Yeltsin before the final dissolution of the Soviet Union was declared on December 25. The two men, however, had promptly agreed on the appointment of a well-known telegenic reformer, Vadim Bakatin, as the new head of the security forces, then in a state of turmoil and uncertainty. According to a Russian journalist, some demoralized KGB officers in the Lubyanka, fearing the worst, had taken to drinking vodka at their desks in a flagrant breach of Chekist discipline.[5]

In bold, lofty rhetoric, the one-time interior minister – only recently dismissed by Gorbachev – outlined his plans to restructure the KGB on the basis of legality and protection of individual rights. And to the ire of his new colleagues, he made a goodwill gesture to the West by giving US ambassador Robert Strauss samples of the extensive electronic eavesdropping equipment previously planted in the Moscow embassy accompanied by charts indicating their location. But wary of instituting a witch hunt – and believing that only a handful of KGB officers were culpable in the conspiracy – Bakatin proceeded cautiously and resisted key personnel changes. His tenure in office as the KGB's final chairman soon ended in frustration, having produced few long-term reforms. Afterwards he openly conceded what had hampered him the most – the lack of a dedicated, like-minded support staff, an overestimation of his own powers, and a failure to infuse the organization with talented administrators drawn from the outside. In a speech delivered at a conference in 1993, Bakatin stated that, while the myth of its invincibility had collapsed, the KGB could not be considered moribund at all.

With the birth of the Russian Federation, Yeltsin had a free hand to create his own security structure. By early 1992, five separate agencies performing the tasks of the defunct KGB had taken shape. Those responsible for electronic eavesdropping and cryptography, for example, became self-contained entities. The largest of all – the Ministestvo Bezopastnosti (Ministry of Security, or MB) – had absorbed no less than 17 major units of its predecessor and was charged primarily with counterintelligence functions. Yeltsin selected a longtime supporter, Colonel General Viktor Barrinakov, as its director. Facing a host of challenges – the growing threat of terrorism posed by ethnic separatists, the pervasiveness of organized crime, and a high degree of demoralization among the rank-and-file – the new director sought to ensure that the MB would enjoy a broad range of powers. In addition, concern was repeatedly voiced by security officials about the intrusion of the Western "special services" in all phases of Russian life.

Yet, the close relationship between the two men came to an end in July 1993, when Yeltsin dismissed Barrinakov from his position, ostensibly for mishandling an attack on Russian border troops between Tadzhikistan and Afghanistan and for violating so-called "ethical norms." Before the end of the year, the Russian president took an even more dramatic step. Maintaining that the entire security system from 1917 to the present had proven "unreformable" and that recent changes were "basically superficial and cosmetic," he proclaimed yet another agency – the Federal'naia Sluzhba Kontrrazvedki (Federal Counterintelligence Service, or FSK). All employees were to be subjected to a "recertification" process that was left unelaborated upon in the edict. Many drew the conclusion that these moves on Yeltsin's part reflected less a desire for genuine reform but a strategy for shoring up his power base with proven loyalists, especially vis-à-vis his parliamentary opponents.

To handle the pressing demands of foreign intelligence, Yeltsin's original security reorganization had established the Sluzhba Vnesheni Razvedki (Russian Foreign Intelligence Service, or SVR). Descended directly from the KGB's First Chief Directorate and maintaining the identical headquarters complex – the "Forest" at Iasenevo – it did not face the same hurdles of public acceptance as its domestic counterparts, whose abuses against Soviet citizens had become the central target of human rights activists, despite the fact of close coordination between the KGB's internal and external wings on many occasions. To head the SVR, Yeltsin turned to a seasoned government figure with an academic reputation, Evgenii Primakov. By 1989, he had become one of Gorbachev's principal foreign policy advisors, having acquired considerable firsthand experience as an envoy in the Middle East. Western officials knew him well, not only because of his vocal support for the invasion and occupation of Afghanistan but also as an apologist for Iraq's Saddam Hussein. When dispatched by Gorbachev on a mission to Washington in May 1991, Primakov easily provoked the disdain of the soon-to-be DCI, Robert Gates. In his view, a person "more personally unwelcome or substantively less qualified" could hardly have been selected.[6]

The SVR immediately put its energy behind a public relations offensive designed to court Western opinion. If questioned, Primakov replied that his prior writings and opinions were simply relics of the past and had no bearing on his current "democratic" outlook. Stressing the basic theme of collaboration rather than confrontation, other SVR officials likewise disavowed prior practices, such as coerced agent recruitment and the cultivation of an "enemy" worldview. In June 1993, Primakov returned to Washington to meet with CIA director James Woolsey to discuss issues related to nuclear proliferation, terrorism, and drug trafficking. Two months later, Woolsey reciprocated by traveling to Moscow for discussions with the heads of both the SVR and the MB. Also on Primakov's itinerary that year were meetings with officials in Germany and the Czech Republic to identify areas of mutual concern. In less publicized actions, intelligence ties with Beijing, severed in 1959, were reestablished, and a new agreement with Cuba allowed an electronic intelligence-gathering facility near Lourdes to remain under Russian control (its closing was announced in 2001 for mostly financial reasons).

To reinforce this new, more benign image, SVR spokesmen pointed to the large number of staff cuts that had occurred as well as the closing of 30 foreign stations, mostly in Africa and small Far Eastern countries. But these reduced figures – dictated by budget cuts and an ailing economy – were deceptive. Many of the foreign intelligence officers who had opted for early retirement continued to work off the books or on a periodic basis as consultants. With more Russians engaging in overseas commerce than ever before, Western counterintelligence found it increasingly difficult to distinguish between actual spies and legitimate businessmen. Further compounding the situation were a significant number of ex-KGB personnel hired by Western firms seeking a foothold in the country. Often making no pretense of their previous careers, they possessed the ability to navigate the complexities of Russian bureaucracy and open doors otherwise closed to outsiders. In many instances as well, relations with their former colleagues in the SVR had not been completely dissolved.

Defections, however, rose sharply and posed a serious problem. Following the failed 1991 coup, the CIA sought to take advantage of the chaotic environment and immediately set up a systematic recruitment plan. For the first time since the beginning of the Cold War, US case officers enjoyed free movement in Moscow without the specter of KGB surveillance and had no difficulty arranging face-to-face meetings with potential recruits depressed about their future prospects. It even brought forth Russian agents from the past – persons who had either been apprehended by Soviet authorities or disappeared from view and who now expected payment for their earlier services. The establishment of the SVR did little to reverse this trend. One major loss to the Americans in early 1992 was Colonel Vladimir Konoplev, who operated under the cover of first secretary at the Russian embassy in Brussels and specialized in scientific-technological espionage. Another defection shortly afterward involved Viktor Oschchencko, who was stationed at the Paris embassy and received asylum in Britain. His disclosures led to the exposure of several French citizens and a British engineer.

In August 1992, a law on foreign intelligence – largely authored by the legal department of the SVR – solidified the dominant position of the president of the Russian Federation. He had sole power to appoint its leaders, formulate strategy, and make all major decisions. The law also spoke of respect for individual rights and forbade the use of intelligence for "antihumanitarian purposes." Despite a section discussing the role of parliamentary oversight, specific enforcement mechanisms were left unmentioned. In a well-received speech delivered at Yasenevo in April 1994, Yeltsin underscored the increasing importance of the SVR in supplying information that would help to secure the country's scientific and technological future. While welcoming improved relations with the West, he also warned against foreign interference that would put Russia's national interest in jeopardy. Revealingly, as well, on December 20, 1995, the SVR took exceptional pride in observing the 75th anniversary of the founding of the Cheka's foreign division. Afterward, it issued a laudatory publication extolling "the large number of glorious deeds" carried out by Soviet foreign intelligence officers "who have made an outstanding contribution to guaranteeing the security of our Homeland."[7]

In a marked departure from past practice, the SVR under Primakov began to assume an assertive role in the conduct of foreign policy. During its entire existence, the KGB had always respected the primacy of the Communist Party and never disseminated its views as a separate body. As NATO's proposed expansion into Central and Eastern Europe started to gain momentum, Primakov circulated a firmly worded statement of opposition – one that directly clashed with the more conciliatory views expressed by the Foreign Ministry. Such an enlargement, he argued, would place a hostile military force in immediate proximity to Russia's borders, causing discontent in the armed forces, and would give sustenance to reactionary, anti-Western groups in the country. Two other controversial issues prompted similar reports by Primakov: the spread of nuclear weapons to several former Soviet states; and the economic and political reintegration of the Commonwealth of Independent States (CIS). When Yeltsin appointed Primakov foreign minister in December 1996, his intelligence connections were by no means abandoned. Several SVR officers accompanied him to his new post, and he remained in regular contact with his successor, Andrei Trubnikov.

In the meantime, grave doubts had arisen about the effectiveness of the domestic service, the FSK, particularly after a failed attack on Grozny, the capital of Chechnya. In December 1994, its disguised forces had been ambushed by separatist Chechen rebels commanded by Major General Dzhokar Dudaev, and its tanks set on fire in the city streets. The following year the FSK became the Federalnaya Sluzhba Bezopasnosti (Federal Security Service, or FSB). But the name change did not prevent the occurrence of another fiasco involving the war against organized Russian crime and the removal of the FSB director.

As the country continued to stagnate with little sense of national resolve and economic conditions worsened, Yeltsin made an appointment in July 1998 that would have significant future consequences. To head the FSB, he selected Vladimir Putin, a little known Kremlin official from St. Petersburg. Despite serving in the KGB for 16 years, he had not risen above the rank of lieutenant colonel and had spent the Gorbachev years posted at a six-man provincial GDR unit in Dresden. Yet, these middling credentials proved no barrier to Putin's rapid rise to political prominence. After only a year directing the FSB, he was appointed prime minister by Yeltsin and, in short order, secured his reputation by responding forcefully to the bombing of two Moscow apartment houses with a new military offensive against the Chechens. Before leaving the FSB, he had told his colleagues, "A few years ago, we succumbed to the illusion that we don't have enemies and we have paid dearly for that."[8]

With Yeltsin's surprise resignation on New Year's Eve 1999, the reins of presidential power passed to Putin – the first officer of the KGB's foreign intelligence division to become the country's leader. Rumors soon circulated that the Kremlin was preparing to consolidate the separate intelligence bodies into a single service reminiscent of the past. Although that failed to occur, Putin showed no hesitation in instituting a series of organizational changes designed to enhance the power and scope of the FSB. The border guards were merged with the security forces, for example, and the surveillance of the military was reinstated to detect any signs of dissension among its members. Unable to absorb its rival, the SVR, the FSB soon possessed its own foreign intelligence operation replete with regional branches. Officially called "organs of external intelligence," it was placed within the security organization's analytical, forecasting, and strategic planning division.

The FSB also found an important new ally in Russian society. Since the earliest days of the Bolsheviks, the KGB had sought to suppress the Russian Orthodox Church – either by direct means or surreptitiously through the widespread recruitment of clergymen as agents and informers. Following the collapse of the Soviet Union, the religious revival came to include, surprisingly enough, a close rapprochement between the FSB and leaders of the clergy. In 2002, the security agency even received its own parish church – the restored fifteenth-century Cathedral of St. Sophia of God's Wisdom located in the courtyard of FSB headquarters on Lubyanka Square (it had served as a storehouse during most of the Soviet period).

At its consecration – attended by FSB head Nikolai Patrushev and other agency officials – Patriarch Aleksi II expressed his hope that the church would help intelligence officers "carry out the difficult work of ensuring the country's security in the face of external and internal ill-wishers, if not enemies."[9] A solemn exchange of gifts took place as well. In concrete terms, this newfound relationship entailed shielding the Orthodox realm against Western proselytizing, whether by the Roman Catholic Church or any Protestant denomination. Putin, himself a practicing Orthodox Christian, paid tribute to the church, calling attention to its "special role in shaping our statehood, our culture, our morals," but also made no secret of his enduring Chekist allegiance, having helped to reinstall a plaque on the Lubyanka in honor of Yuri Andropov. As a precaution, it had been removed by KGB personnel the evening that witnessed the toppling of the Dzerzhinsky statue.

For the United States, the end of the Cold War meant the dissolution of a key component – the CIA's Soviet/East European Division. Replacing it was the Central Eurasian Task Force, which evolved into the Central Eurasian Division. But its thinly staffed stations in regions such as Turkestan and Uzbekistan held little interest for the senior echelon at headquarters. On the intellectual front, the CIA decided to end its covert financial support for magazines, academic journals, books, and videos produced by Soviet bloc expatriates based in Western Europe – a decidedly "bittersweet parting" in the words of one ranking official.[10] Conceived at the beginning of the Cold War, the program had become increasingly sophisticated over the years, especially in the art of smuggling miniaturized copies of the Bible, Alexsandr Solzhenitsyn's *Gulag Archipelago*, and other banned works into countries behind the iron curtain. Direct funding of Radio Free Europe/Radio Liberty (RFE/RL) by the CIA had ended in 1971 and was rerouted through congressional legislation. After 1989 – at the urging of Vaclav Havel and other leading figures – RFE/RL established local bureaus throughout its broadcast region to assist with the democratic transition. As the Czech president stated, "We need your professionalism and your ability to see events from a broad perspective."[11]

Feeling assured that direct threats to the United States had diminished in the immediate post-Cold War period, the CIA embarked on an accelerated program of declassifying documents under the general rubric of openness. It took, however, the pressure of Senator Daniel Patrick Moynihan to persuade US officials to initiate the release of the nearly 3,000 decrypted messages of the Venona project. In 1943, fearing that the Soviet Union might conclude a separate peace treaty with Nazi Germany, the US Army's Signals Intelligence Service (which evolved into the NSA) attempted to monitor Soviet diplomatic cablegrams leaving and entering the country. Not until three years later when Soviet code clerks carelessly began to use the unbreakable one-time pads multiple times was a readable text obtained.

American officials were astonished to see that nearly half of the subject matter dealt with espionage, not diplomatic affairs. Although only a fraction of the intelligence traffic was deciphered – and Moscow later learned of the project through two of its spies – the penetration of virtually every major US government agency of military or diplomatic importance now appeared a well-documented fact. Nearly 350 citizens, immigrants, and permanent residents of the United States were found to have a covert connection to Soviet espionage; roughly half were known by their real names, the other half by their cover names. The identity of more than 100 agents residing in other Western countries also came to light (the British had joined the project in the late 1940s).

But for a variety of reasons, the general public was never made aware of Venona until the joint announcement by the FBI, CIA, and NSA in 1995. Within the government, too, it constituted a highly compartmentalized secret. President Truman learned only about the substance of the messages, not about the project itself, while the CIA remained in the dark until 1952. In retrospect, this exceptional degree of secrecy exacted a high price. Several historians maintain that the Cold War, in all likelihood, would have taken a very different course had knowledge of Venona been more widely disseminated at the time.[12] Besides helping the American public gain a sounder understanding of the Soviet threat, it could have affected the trials of Alger Hiss and the Rosenbergs by introducing crucial pieces of evidence. In fact, only 15 percent of the Soviet agents identified by the Venona decrypts ever faced prosecution, primarily because authorities feared their use in an American court of law would compromise the project.[13]

For the present, however, the most pressing question was how the United States would adapt to a new post-Cold War era. Little consensus existed. At the swearing-in ceremony for the new DCI, Robert Gates, in November 1991, President George H. W. Bush told the audience at Langley that the intelligence community would have to change "as rapidly and profoundly as the world itself has changed."[14] Reflecting the fundamental reversal in US–Soviet relations that had taken place, Gates became the first CIA chief to travel to Moscow and visit the foreign intelligence headquarters at Yasenevo. As the first career analyst ever to head the agency – and a critic of the excessive bureaucratization of both the analytical and operational branches – he readily embarked on an ambitious reform program by appointing more than a dozen wide-ranging task forces composed of both agency personnel and consumers. But hardly had they completed their reports than the 1992 presidential election brought an end to the Bush administration and Gates's brief tenure as DCI.

A period of drift followed. Any reforms that occurred were *ad hoc* in nature, lacking urgency as well as a larger strategic vision. Upon assuming office, the new president, William Jefferson Clinton, evinced little interest in intelligence and foreign affairs. He soon cancelled the daily oral briefing and maintained only distant contact with his new DCI, R. James Woolsey, Jr., a Washington lawyer and former undersecretary of the US Navy. Despite his attempts to focus public attention on the CIA's substantive work, he became a casualty of the Aldrich Ames affair by not taking sufficiently strong disciplinary action against the superiors of the long-time Soviet mole. Woolsey's successor, John M.

Deutch, an ex-deputy secretary of defense, demanded and received cabinet status, but he fared even worse and departed in 1996. At a time when greater penetration into hard targets such as terrorist cells and nuclear weapons proliferators was being urged, Deutch aroused much ridicule because of his stipulation that a foreign recruitment could not occur without the approval of the person's human rights and criminal record by senior officers. He was also found guilty by the CIA inspector general of mishandling national security information on his home computers.

Beyond this rapid turnover at the top – five different directors within the space of nine years – the so-called "peace dividend" translated into a considerable downsizing of the CIA staff – roughly 25 percent from its height of nearly 22,000 employees during the Reagan years. Noticeably affected was the clandestine service, as many mid-level officers, seeing little opportunity for advancement, chose to retire and new training classes numbered in the single digits. In 1992, yet another thorny issue came to the fore when the CIA concluded a "glass ceiling" study that showed women's achievements in the Directorate of Operations failed to receive the same degree of recognition as those of their male colleagues. In addition, a female case officer initiated a class action lawsuit, which the CIA settled in 1995 through a combination of financial reimbursement and retroactive assignments. But by no means did it bring an end to the argument over gender discrimination and sexual harassment.

Another critique held that the CIA had gone astray by developing a "risk averse" culture. In the clandestine service, for example, the relationship between headquarters management and officers in the field had shifted in favor of the former, leaving the latter with greatly diminished authority. As one case officer complained, "Operations that made sense in the field – that is where the potential gain outweighed the risk – did not make sense in the Washington environment. Headquarters came to have the first and final say on operations."[15] In March 1995, Robert Baer – one of the agency's few Arabic-speaking case officers – was in the midst of planning a covert action with opponents of Saddam Hussein in northern Iraq when he found himself the target of an FBI investigation set in motion by the Clinton White House.[16] His presumed offense involved running a rogue operation and plotting the assassination of the Iraqi dictator – a violation of Executive Order 12333. Recalled to Washington, Baer passed a polygraph test with no difficulty, and the unsupported charges were eventually dropped. The CIA, however, declined to aid his defense, claiming that such investigations had become a commonplace occurrence.

This decade of drift came to an abrupt halt with the surprise terrorist attacks on September 11, 2001. Some 3,000 people were killed in less than two hours as passenger jets hijacked by Islamist extremists crashed into the Pentagon and the twin towers of the World Trade Center. In a widely seen television interview shortly afterward, Vice President Dick Cheney emphasized the need for "robust intelligence programs … to work the dark side, if you will. We've got to spend time in the shadows of the intelligence world. A lot that needs to be done will have to be done quietly, without any discussion, using sources and methods that are available to our intelligence agencies."[17] As the CIA began to reorder its priorities under this imperative, a strong wave of nostalgia for the Cold War could be detected at Langley. An earlier comment by James Woolsey made during his Senate confirmation hearings summed up the mood. "We have slain a large dragon," he said. "But we live now in a jungle filled with a bewildering variety of poisonous snakes. And in many ways, the dragon was easier to keep track of."[18] Several influential political scientists echoed this refrain as well. A bipolar world centered on Washington and Moscow – it was argued – possessed an unusual degree of stability and predictability, making it far more manageable than the daunting mixture of terrorist groups and intransigent states that replaced it.

Yet, such a view appears overly myopic, as it ignores many of the most salient characteristics of the Cold War. Never before had the world seen a contest of arms on such an immense and threatening scale. An estimated 20,000 missiles were aimed at each other, often placed on high alert and subject to human error at all times. Its costs reached staggering sums, more than US$2 trillion for the Americans alone. Pitting fundamentally irreconcilable ideologies against one another, the Cold War was also a conflict that permeated distant regions of the Third World. Nor was the ultimate outcome guaranteed in favor of the West. In the 1970s, the conviction grew on both sides that the Soviets and their surrogates – displaying increasing self-confidence – were on the march while the United States and its allies had been forced into a position of military and psychological retreat. An influential French journalist and analyst, Jean-François Revel, doubted whether democracies themselves, owing to their essentially inward orientation, had the ability to mount an effective defense against those seeking their annihilation.[19]

Strategic intelligence helped to shape this struggle in a profound and sometimes contradictory manner. Beginning with the advent of the U-2 spy plane, the technological revolution in imagery intelligence allowed each side to monitor the other's nuclear strike force, thereby reducing uncertainty and error and providing a stabilizing element in diplomatic negotiations and arms control agreements. At the same time, the Soviet Union displayed a ruthless determination to acquire

Western technological and scientific secrets via espionage. Its striking success in this endeavor was mirrored in the fact that by the early 1980s – according to a Pentagon estimate – nearly 70 percent of the Warsaw Pact's weapons systems were based in varying degrees on US designs.[20] The revelation of individual spy cases reinforced each side's more sinister suspicions of the other throughout the period. One must also be careful not to measure the KGB's activities solely by a Western yardstick. Many of its foreign operations aimed not just at obtaining information but at silencing dissent against the regime in whatever form it appeared – whether involving an émigré writer, dancer, musician, or chess player – leading one analyst to label the Soviet Union, first and foremost, a "counterintelligence state."[21]

Probably the most enduring legacy left by the Cold War was the realization that intelligence organizations play an indispensable role in the structure of a modern nation. As once noted by the former diplomat and deputy DCI Vernon Walters, "Shrinking distances and time factors compel decision-making at a far faster rate than we have known in the past."[22] In addition, such decisions are often more complex and far-reaching in their consequences, thus making the possession of maximum knowledge all the more imperative. The case of the United States is especially instructive. Since the days of George Washington and Thomas Jefferson, Americans have engaged in periodic espionage – the Continental Congress already appropriated the first funds for intelligence purposes in November 1776[23] – but a deep-seated aversion existed in the culture, as many regarded covert activity as alien to the high ethical principles professed by the country. The arduous experience of waging the silent struggle of the Cold War caused a fundamental shift in this attitude, and major institutions came into existence as a result. Controversies will doubtlessly persist regarding the proper scope and conduct of peacetime intelligence, yet its necessity in a world still riddled with conflict and intrigue now seems beyond dispute.

Notes

1 Joachim Gauck, *Die Stasi-Akten: Das unheimliche Erbe der DDR* (Reinbek bei Hamburg: Rowohlt, 1991), 97.
2 Nadya Nedelsky, "Czechoslovakia, and the Czech and Slovak Republics," in Lavina Stan (Ed.), *Transitional Justice in Eastern Europe and the Former Soviet Union: Reckoning with the Communist Past* (Abingdon, Oxon, UK: Routledge, 2008), 49.
3 Cited by Kieran Williams, "The Czech Republic Since 1993," in Kieran Williams and Dennis Deletant (Eds), *Security Intelligence Services in New Democracies: The Czech Republic, Slovakia and Romania* (New York, NY: Palgrave Macmillan, 2000), 83.

4 *Manchester Guardian*, June 19, 2002.

5 Yevgenia Albats, *The State Within a State: The KGB and Its Hold on Russia – Past, Present, and Future* (New York, NY: Farrar, Straus and Giroux. 1994), 295.

6 Robert M., Gates, *From the Shadows: The Ultimate Insider's Story of Five Presidents and How They Won the Cold War* (New York, NY: Simon and Schuster, 1996), 502.

7 Christopher Andrew and Vasili Mitrokhin, *The Sword and the Shield: The Mitrokhin Archive and the Secret History of the KGB* (New York, NY: Basic Books, 1999), 565.

8 *Economist*, August 23, 2007.

9 *Moscow Times*, March 8, 2002.

10 Milt Bearden and James Risen, *The Main Enemy: The Inside Story of the CIA's Final Showdown with the KGB* (New York, NY: Random House, 2003), 428. See also Alfred A. Reisch, *Hot Books in the Cold War: The CIA-Funded Secret Western Book Distribution Program Behind the Iron Curtain* (Budapest, Hungary: Central European University Press, 2013).

11 See http://www.rferl.org/info/history/133.html. See also Arch Puddington, *Broadcasting Freedom: The Cold War Triumph of Radio Free Europe and Radio Liberty* (Lexington, KY: University Press of Kentucky, 2003).

12 See John Earl Haynes and Harvey Klehr, *Venona: Decoding Soviet Espionage in America* (New Haven, CT: Yale University Press, 1999), 8–22.

13 Matthew M. Aid, *Silent Sentry: The Untold Story of the National Security Agency* (New York, NY: Bloomsbury Press, 2009), 23.

14 Cited by Christopher Andrew, *For the President's Eyes Only: Secret Intelligence and the American Presidency from Washington to Bush* (New York, NY: HarperCollins, 1995), 532.

15 Melissa Boyle Mahle, *Denial and Deception: An Insider's View of the CIA from Iran-Contra to 9/11* (New York, NY: Nation Books, 2004), 182.

16 See Robert Baer, *See No Evil: The True Story of a Ground Soldier in the CIA's War on Terrorism* (New York, NY: Crown Publishers, 2002).

17 Dick Cheney, *In My Time: A Personal and Political History* (New York, NY: Simon and Schuster, 2011), 335.

18 *New York Times*, February 3, 1993.

19 Jean-François Revel, *How Democracies Perish* (New York, NY: HarperCollins, 1985).

20 Andrew and Mitrokhin, *The Sword and the Shield*, 557.

21 John J. Dziak, *Chekisty: A History of the KGB* (Lexington, MA: Lexington Books, 1987).

22 Vernon A. Walters, *Silent Missions* (Garden City, NY: Doubleday, 1978), 621.

23 Stephen F. Knott, *Secret and Sanctioned: Covert Operations and the American Presidency* (New York, NY: Oxford University Press, 1996), 14.

Glossary

active measures: A Soviet term for political manipulation and propaganda designed to impact both hostile and neutral countries.

agent: A person, usually a foreign national, who has been recruited by a case officer from an intelligence service to perform undercover missions.

agent of influence: An individual, usually in an important government or media position, who attempts to influence policy rather than collect intelligence.

agent provocateur: An operative dispatched to incite a target group or individual to action in order to discredit them.

asset: A clandestine resource, normally an agent.

black bag operation: A CIA term for an under-the-table transaction, such as funding a foreign political party.

black propaganda: Propaganda that claims to emanate from a source other than the true one.

blowback: A deception planted abroad by an intelligence agency that returns to the originating country and gains credibility.

bona fides: An individual's verified qualifications, credentials, or background history.

case officer: A professional member of an intelligence agency directly responsible for giving instructions and direction to an assigned agent.

cell: The lowest and most expendable unit in an espionage network.

Chekist: A member of the original Soviet security organization, the Cheka, now used as an honorific for Russian intelligence officers.

chief of station: The top CIA officer stationed in a foreign country, either officially recognized by the host country or working surreptitiously in violation of its law – the equivalent of a KGB resident or SIS head of station.

code name: An alias used by a spy for reasons of security or a word or term assigned to a program or operation, which may or may not be classified.

COMINT: Communications intelligence, usually collected by technical interception and code breaking, but also by employing human agents.

conspiratorial work: The preferred Marxist-Leninist term for the art and practices of espionage.

courier: A messenger responsible for the secure transmission and delivery of secret material for an intelligence organization, sometimes unaware of the fact.

covert action: Clandestine activities that are designed to be difficult or impossible to trace back to the sponsoring intelligence organization.

cryptanalysis: The art of "breaking" codes or ciphers and rendering them into plain (or readable) text.

cryptogram: A message in code or cipher.

cryptography: The development of techniques that will safeguard a text from an unauthorized recipient.

dead drop: A prearranged hiding place where material can be left undetected for another party to retrieve, typically parks, cemeteries, bridges, railway station lockers, and cracks in walls.

decrypt: A deciphered or decoded message.

defector: A person with intelligence value who volunteers to work for another intelligence service, either requesting asylum or staying in place.

disinformation: The creation and dissemination of misleading or inaccurate information in order to darken the reputation of the targeted enemy.

double agent: An agent who is under the control of another intelligence service and is being used against the original service.

ELINT: Electronic intelligence, usually collected by technical interception such as telemetry from a rocket launch collected by receivers at a distance.

executive action: A CIA euphemism for targeted assassination.

exfiltration: A clandestine rescue operation designed to remove a defector, refugee, or agent from a dangerous situation, often including the person's family.

false flag: The deliberate misrepresentation by a recruiter to gain a more favorable reception by a potential agent.

floater: A person used for a one-time or occasional low-level intelligence operation.

gray propaganda: Propaganda without any identifiable source or author.

handler: See case officer.

head of station: The British equivalent of a CIA chief of station or KGB resident.

honey trap: A slang phrase designating the use of men or women to stage compromising sexual situations.

HUMINT: Intelligence collected by human sources such as agents.

illegal: An operative infiltrated into a targeted country under a false identity and without the protection of diplomatic immunity.

IMINT: Image intelligence, usually acquired by high-altitude planes or space vehicles.

infiltration: The placement of an agent in a targeted area or group.

legend: A false identity concocted for an intelligence operative.

meal ticket: An expression used by intelligence professionals for valuable information supplied by a defector in return for resettlement.

microdot: A photograph of a document or image reduced to the size of a period at the end of a sentence. The modern technique originated in interwar Germany.

mighty Wurlitzer: A term coined by Frank Wisner of the CIA to describe its widespread intelligence-gathering and propaganda network in the early Cold War.

mirror-imaging: The assessment of an unfamiliar situation by drawing analogies from familiar ones, regarded by intelligence professionals as a seriously flawed procedure.

mole: A human penetration into an intelligence service or other high-security organizations, often a defector who has agreed to work in place. The term originated in seventeenth-century England.

music box: A KGB term for a radio transmitter.

National Intelligence Estimate (NIE): A CIA evaluation of national security concerns, usually presented to the National Security Council.

noise: A mass of information that obscures vital data and later proves irrelevant.

Non-official cover (NOC): A CIA case officer operating without diplomatic cover, similar to an Eastern bloc illegal.

notional agent: A fictitious agent normally used to convey fabricated information.

nugget: A British term for an enticement offered to a potential defector.

one-time pad: An unbreakable cipher system for transmitting secret messages.

open code: A cryptographic system whose external text possesses a real meaning in order to disguise the actual hidden meaning.

operative: An intelligence officer or agent operating in the field.

overflight: A mission by a spy plane equipped with cameras to collect strategic intelligence about a targeted country.

Piscine: A nickname for the French intelligence and counter-intelligence service owing to the close proximity of its headquarters to a swimming pool.

plumbing: A CIA term describing the operational support system necessary in a foreign locale, ranging from safe houses and dead drops to couriers and technical specialists.

President's Daily Brief (PDB): The CIA summary delivered to the president every morning and accompanied by a senior officer.

resident: The top KGB officer stationed in a foreign country, either officially recognized by the host country or working surreptitiously in violation of its law – the equivalent of a CIA chief of station and SIS head of station.

residentura: The Russian term for an espionage office or staff in a foreign country.

Romeo spy: A male intelligence officer who seduces female secretaries and professionals for purposes of espionage – a specialty of the former East German service.

safe house: A residence maintained by an intelligence service for clandestine meetings, often between an agent and handler, or for hiding a defector.

SIGINT: Signals intelligence or the combination of COMINT and ELINT into one unit of intelligence-gathering dealing with all electronic emanations and transmissions.

sleeper: A spy assigned to a target area to be activated at a future time.

special tasks: A Russian intelligence term for assassinations, kidnapping, and sabotage operations.

spy dust: A harmless chemical marking compound developed by the KGB for tracking the activities of Western diplomats and military attachés.

swallow: A Russian term for a female operative who gains information through sexual activity or stages a situation for potential blackmail.

TECHINT: Technical intelligence concerning the weapons and equipment used by foreign nations.

tradecraft: The methods employed by intelligence officers to conduct their operations without being detected by the opposing intelligence service.

Treff: A German term used internationally designating a confidential meeting between the case officer and agent.

triple agent: An agent who works for three intelligence organizations but withholds significant information from the other two at the insistence of the third service. Also an agent who is dispatched with the objective of being recruited by an adversary but who then becomes a double agent for the original service.

walk-in: A person who volunteers to spy for an opposition government, often by entering an official installation without previous contact, and requesting political asylum or agreeing to work in place.

walking the cat: An American term for the thorough review of a failed operation from its very beginning.

wet affairs: A Russian slang term for intelligence operations that involve the death of the targeted person.

wilderness of mirrors: A phrase of T. S. Eliot invoked by James Angleton of the CIA to describe the vast complexity and confusion inherent in the world of espionage.

Chronology

1945	June	The FBI apprehends six suspected spies associated with the pro-communist magazine *Amerasia*.
	September	Igor Gouzenko defects to Canadian officials in Ottawa.
	November	Elizabeth Bentley agrees to cooperate with the FBI in identifying US government officials as Soviet spies.
1946	March	Winston Churchill delivers his "Iron Curtain" speech in Fulton, Missouri.
1947	July	The National Security Act establishes the CIA.
	December	The National Security Council authorizes the CIA to conduct covert action.
1948	August	Whittaker Chambers testifies before the House Committee on Un-American Activities.
1949	January	Beijing falls to the forces of Mao Zedong.
	April	The North Atlantic Treaty Organization (NATO) is formed.
	May	The 11-month Berlin Airlift successfully ends.
	August	The Soviet Union explodes its first atomic bomb.
		East European spy trials commence.
	September	Konrad Adenauer is elected first chancellor of West Germany.
1950	January	Alger Hiss is found guilty of perjury.
	February	The East German Ministry of State Security is formed.
		US Senator Joseph McCarthy publicly claims the existence of communist spies in the State Department.
		Klaus Fuchs pleads guilty to having violated the British Official Secrets Act.
	June	North Korea invades South Korea.
1951	May	Guy Burgess and Donald Maclean defect to the Soviet Union.

(continued)

1952	March	Ian Fleming completes his first James Bond novel, *Casino Royale.*
	September	Isser Harel becomes Mossad chief.
1953	March	Joseph Stalin dies.
	June	Julius and Ethel Rosenberg are executed as communist spies in New York.
	July	Soviet security head Lavrenti Beria is tried and executed for treason.
		Armistice ends the Korean War.
	August	A CIA-assisted coup overthrows Iranian Premier Mohammed Mossadeq.
1954	June	Guatemalan President Jacobo Arbenz is ousted with CIA cooperation.
	December	James Angleton becomes the CIA's first counterintelligence chief.
1955	April	NATO, or the Atlantic Alliance, is established for the collective military defense of its members.
	May	The Berlin Tunnel is completed under CIA–SIS direction.
		The State Treaty of Austria proclaims the country's neutrality, and the occupying powers depart.
		The Warsaw Pact is formed as a rival collective security body.
1956	February	Nikita Khrushchev delivers a secret speech denouncing Stalin.
	April	The West German foreign intelligence service is established under Reinhard Gehlen.
	July	The United States dispatches the first U-2 surveillance flight over the Soviet Union from Wiesbaden, Germany.
		The Suez Crisis begins.
	December	Israel and West Germany establish intelligence relations prior to diplomatic recognition eight years later.
1957	October	The USSR successfully launches Sputnik I satellite.
1959	January	Fidel Castro assumes power in Cuba.
	June	Klaus Fuchs is released from prison and becomes an East German citizen.
	November	President Dwight Eisenhower lays the cornerstone of the new CIA headquarters at Langley, Virginia.
1960	May	The U-2 piloted by Francis Gary Powers is shot down over Sverdlovsk, Russia.
		Adolf Eichmann is captured in Argentina by the Israeli Mossad.

(continued)

	August	The US launches its first successful CORONA photoreconnaissance satellite mission.
	December	Cuba openly aligns itself with the Soviet Union.
1961	April	Cuba repels US-backed exile force at the Bay of Pigs.
	August	East Germany begins construction of the Berlin Wall to prevent a further population exodus.
		The Defense Intelligence Agency is established under the US Secretary of Defense.
	September	The National Reconnaissance Office is formed to oversee all satellite and overflight projects whether overt or covert.
		Oleg Penkovsky of the GRU is recruited by Western intelligence.
	November	Heinz Felfe of the BND is arrested as a KGB spy.
	December	Antoli Golitsyn defects to the West.
1962	February	Rudolf Abel and Francis Gary Powers are traded in the first Cold War spy exchange.
	October	The first James Bond film *Dr. No* premieres in London.
		A U-2 overflight of Cuba detects Soviet nuclear missiles capable of striking the US mainland.
1963	May	Soviets execute Colonel Oleg Penkovsky of the GRU as a US collaborator.
	July	The USSR grants Kim Philby political asylum and Soviet citizenship.
	September	John le Carré's *The Spy Who Came in from the Cold* is published.
	November	South Vietnamese President Ngo Dinh Diem is assassinated.
		US President John F. Kennedy is assassinated by Lee Harvey Oswald.
1964	February	Yuri Nosenko defects to the United States.
	October	The KGB helps force the resignation of Nikita Khrushchev.
	November	Richard Sorge is posthumously made a Hero of the Soviet Union.
1965	July	The first US troops are sent to Vietnam.
1967	April	Yuri Andropov begins his 15-year tenure as KGB chief.
	June	Israel defeats Arab forces in the Six-Day War.
1968	January	The Tet Offensive undermines US popular support of the Vietnam War.

(continued)

	August	The Prague Spring reform movement is suppressed by troops of the Warsaw Pact.
1969	April	Yuri Nosenko is cleared by the United States of being a Soviet spy.
1971	June	The "Pentagon Papers" become public.
	September	The British government orders a mass expulsion of KGB/GRU personnel from London.
1972	February	US President Richard Nixon visits the People's Republic of China.
1973	September	The Allende government in Chile is overthrown.
	October	Israeli intelligence fails to detect the outbreak of the Yom Kippur War.
1974	April	Günter Guillaume and his wife are arrested as East German spies in Bonn.
	August	President Richard Nixon announces his resignation.
	December	A *New York Times* exposé sparks a major investigation of the CIA.
1975	January	Philip Agee makes public the names of roughly 250 CIA operatives.
	April	South Vietnam falls to the communists.
	December	CIA station chief Richard Welch is assassinated in Athens, Greece.
1976	February	Cuban and Soviet forces help to install a communist government in Angola.
1978	July	Ion Pacepa of Romanian intelligence defects to the United States.
	September	Bulgarian dissident Georgi Markov is murdered in London.
	October	John Paul II is elected pope.
1979	November	Anthony Blunt is publicly exposed as a former communist spy and stripped of his knighthood.
		The Iranian hostage crisis begins following the overthrow of the shah.
	December	Soviet troops are dispatched to Afghanistan.
1980	August	Solidarity is formed in Poland under the leadership of Lech Wałesa.
1981	October	Anwar Sadat of Egypt is murdered by Muslim extremists.
	December	Martial law is declared in Poland.
1983	May	President Ronald Reagan announces US support for anti-Sandinista forces.

(continued)

	September	A Soviet fighter pilot downs KAL flight 007, killing all on board.
	November	The Able Archer NATO exercise causes high alarm among Soviet officials.
1985	May	Members of the John Walker spy ring are arrested by the FBI.
	July	Greenpeace's *Rainbow Warrior* is sunk by the French in a New Zealand harbor.
1986	February	Larry Wu-tai Chin commits suicide after being found guilty of espionage for the People's Republic of China.
	April	La Belle Discothèque in West Berlin is bombed by Libyan operatives.
	May	Jonathan Jay Pollard pleads guilty to passing information to Israel.
	August	Edward Lee Howard becomes the first CIA defector and is granted political asylum in the Soviet Union.
1989	April	Solidarity is legalized and enters the Polish election.
	September	Hungary becomes independent.
	November	The Berlin Wall falls.
	December	The communist regimes in Czechoslovakia, Bulgaria, and Romania are toppled.
1990	April	The KGB admits responsibility for the 1940 Katyn massacre of Polish officers.
	May	Boris Yeltsin is elected president of Russia.
	October	Joachim Gauck is named administrator for the voluminous Stasi files.
1991	January	Helmut Kohl is elected first chancellor of reunified Germany.
	September	The KGB is abolished and replaced by several new entities.
	November	Robert Gates begins a post-Cold War reorganization of the CIA.
	December	The new Russian foreign intelligence service is created.
		The Soviet Union splits into the Commonwealth of Independent States.
1992	November	Vasili Mitrokhin defects to the British with his secret KGB archive.
	December	Stella Rimington, the first woman to head a leading government security agency, becomes chief of MI5.

(continued)

1993	November	NATO spy Rainer Rupp receives 12-year prison sentence in Germany.
1994	February	Aldrich Ames of the CIA is arrested for spying for Russia.
1995	July	Soviet messages deciphered by the Venona project are made public.
	October	The prison sentence of East German foreign intelligence chief Markus Wolf is overturned.
1998	July	Vladimir Putin is named head of Russia's Federal Security Service.
1999	September	Melita Norwood acknowledges her identity as Britain's longest serving Soviet spy.
2000	March	Vladimir Putin is elected President of Russia.
2001	February	FBI-agent Robert Hanssen is apprehended as a Soviet spy.
	September	Four coordinated terrorist attacks are launched by al-Qaeda against the United States.

Suggested Further Reading

Aldrich, Richard J., *The Hidden Hand: Britain, America, and Cold War Secret Intelligence* (London: John Murray, 2001).

Andrew, Christopher M., *For the President's Eyes Only: Secret Intelligence and the American Presidency from Washington to Bush* (New York, NY: HarperCollins, 1995).

——*Defending the Realm: The Authorized History of MI5* (New York, NY: Knopf, 2009).

Andrew, Christopher M. and Oleg Gordievsky, *KGB: The Inside Story of Its Foreign Operations from Lenin to Gorbachev* (New York, NY: HarperCollins, 1990).

Andrew, Christopher M. and Vasili Mitrokhin, *The Sword and the Shield: The Mitrokhin Archive and the Secret History of the KGB* (New York, NY: Basic Books, 1999).

Barrett, David M. and Max Holland, *Blind Over Cuba: The Photo Gap and the Missile Crisis* (College Station, TX: Texas A&M University Press, 2012).

Bozeman, Adda B., *Strategic Statecraft and Intelligence* (New York, NY: Brassey's (US), 1991).

Brugioni, Dino A., *Eyeball to Eyeball: The Inside Story of the Cuban Missile Crisis* (New York, NY: Random House, 1992).

——*Eyes in the Sky: Eisenhower, the CIA, and Cold War Aerial Espionage* (Annapolis, MD: Naval Institute Press, 2010).

Chapman, James, *Licence to Thrill: A Cultural History of the James Bond Films*, second edition (London: I. B. Tauris, 2007).

Gates, Robert, *From the Shadows: The Ultimate Insider's Story of Five Presidents and How They Won the Cold War* (New York, NY: Simon and Schuster, 1996).

Gieseke, Jens, *The History of the Stasi: East Germany's Secret Police, 1945–1990* (New York, NY: Berghahn Books, 2014).

Harrington, Stuart A., *Spies Among Us: Inside a Spycatcher's World* (Novato, CA: Presidio Press, 1999).

Haynes, John Earl and Harvey Klehr, *Venona: Decoding Soviet Espionage in America* (New Haven, CT: Yale University Press, 1999).

——*Early Cold War Spies: The Espionage Trials that Shaped American Politics* (Cambridge: Cambridge University Press, 2006).

Haynes, John Earl, Harvey Klehr, and Alexander Vassiliev, *Spies: The Rise and Fall of the KGB in America* (New Haven, CT: Yale University Press, 2009).

Helms, Richard with William Hood, *A Look Over My Shoulder: A Life in the Central Intelligence Agency* (New York, NY: Random House, 2003).

Hitz, Frederick P., *The Great Game: The Myths and Realties of Espionage* (New York, NY: Alfred A. Knopf, 2004).

Kalugin, Oleg with Fen Montaigne, *The First Directorate: My 32 Years in Intelligence and Espionage Against the West* (New York, NY: St. Martin's Press, 1994).

Lamphere, Robert with Tom Shachtman, *The FBI–KGB War: A Special Agent's Story* (New York, NY: Random House, 1986).

Macrakis, Kristie, *Seduced by Secrets: Inside the Stasi's Spy-Tech World* (Cambridge, MA: Cambridge University Press, 2008).

Murphy, David E., Sergei A. Kondrashev, and George Bailey, *Battleground Berlin: CIA vs KGB in the Cold War* (New Haven, CT: Yale University Press, 1997).

Puddington, Arch, *Broadcasting Freedom: The Cold War Triumph of Radio Free Europe and Radio Liberty* (Lexington, KY: University Press of Kentucky, 2003).

Reisch, Alfred A., *Hot Books in the Cold War. The CIA-Funded Secret Western Book Distribution Program behind the Iron Curtain* (Budapest, Hungary: Central European University Press, 2013).

Richelson, Jeffrey T., *The US Intelligence Community*, 6th edition (Boulder, CO: Westview Press, 2011).

Soldatov, Andrei and Irina Borogan, *The New Nobility: The Restoration of Russia's Security State and the Enduring Legacy of the KGB* (New York, NY: Public Affairs, 2011).

Stafford, David, *Spies Beneath Berlin* (London: John Murray, 2002).

Stiller, Werner with Jefferson Adams, *Beyond the Wall: Memoirs of an East and West German Spy* (New York, NY: Brassey's (US), 1992).

Tanenhaus, Sam, *Whittaker Chambers: A Biography* (New York, NY: Random House, 1997).

Wallace, Robert and H. Keith Melton with Henry Robert Schlesinger, *Spycraft: The Secret History of the CIA's Spytechs, from Communism to Al-Qaeda* (London: Penguin Group, 2008).

Weinstein, Allen and Alexander Vassiliev, *The Haunted Wood: Soviet Espionage in America – The Stalin Era* (New York, NY: Random House, 1999).

Weiser, Benjamin, *A Secret Life: The Polish Officer, His Covert Mission, and the Price He Paid to Save His Country* (New York, NY: Public Affairs, 2004).

Wise, David, *Spy: The Inside Story of How the FBI's Robert Hanssen Betrayed America* (New York, NY: Random House, 2002).

Wolf, Markus with Anne McElvoy, *Man Without a Face: The Autobiography of Communism's Greatest Spymaster* (New York, NY: Times Books, 1997).

Index

164   *Index*

Made in the USA
Las Vegas, NV
08 May 2023

71754222R00098